SECURITY TEAM OPERATING SYSTEM

How to Run an Unstoppable Team

CHRISTIAN HYATT

STONE CREST
Stone Crest Publishing
www.stonecrestbooks.com

Security Team Operating System © Copyright 2024 Christian Hyatt
First Edition

Published in the United States by Stone Crest Books
Stone Crest Books | www.stonecrestbooks.com
An imprint of Dinosaur House

ISBN: 978-1-961462-17-5 (hardcover)
         978-1-961462-18-2 (paperback)
         978-1-961462-19-9 (ebook)

Executive Editor: Chas Hoppe
Publishing Manager: Stone Crest Books

Contents

FOREWORD

The single biggest barrier to implementing strategy is courage. What makes superstar managers so impressive is not what they are doing but the fact that they are doing it at all.

Many people (and firms) lack the guts to stick with the plans and goals they have set for themselves. They lack the courage of their own convictions.

—David A. Maister, "The Courage to Manage"

When Christian asked me to write the foreword to this book, I was excited at the opportunity. After all, I can provide a lot of context as his business partner at risk3sixty for almost a decade, as of this writing. I could tell a lot of stories—ten years is plenty of time to build good stories. Maybe that is for a different book.

As it relates to this book, I want to share some context that may be helpful to you, the reader—specifically, some things that Christian may not volunteer about himself.

Let's start with the bottom line up front:

1. **The Security Team Operating System works!** We have been coaching clients and helping them implement this system for years, and to great effect. This is not theory. This is our proven method to practically build and run a world-class security team. We have also implemented the same "Management Operating System" to run our business at risk3sixty. We know it works because we have scaled our company and security teams across the nation using it.

2. **Why would Christian write and publish this?** The Security Team Operating System represents a portion of our previously unpublished

1

intellectual property. We know this system works; we confidently implement it for clients every day. Christian wanted to publish this as a way to serve our security community and move the needle for infosec leaders by equipping them with practical guidance to build and run great teams. Realistically, we cannot serve every potential client that needs help here—this book is an attempt to serve those thousands of security leaders and their organizations that may never become clients of risk3sixty.

3. **Why read this book?** Business theory is great if you like that stuff, but it has limited value if not also actionable. This book is actionable and will save you a lot of time in setting up a team operating system. Digesting this material and implementing a form of this operating system in your organization will make you a better and more effective leader, period. It will mature and accelerate your thinking and enable you to be more confident in championing change and getting the program support that you need.

Now that we've got the bottom line out of the way, allow me to provide that context I promised.

I first met Christian in 2015 during our executive MBA program at Georgia Tech University. As I recall, we met on the first day and decided to sit next to each other since we shared a first name. We later became project partners for most of our classes and then eventually decided to become business partners when we founded risk3sixty.

One of the first things I recognized quickly about Christian was that he was a thought leader and a value creator. Christian was not only a subject matter expert in the cybersecurity space, but he had strong, well-considered, and original thoughts and opinions that often departed from the typical overused industry talking points. He could then articulate those thoughts and opinions logically and progressively to educate people who previously knew nothing about that particular topic.

It was masterful to watch, and, to me, seemingly rare to be able to take deep original thought on a subject and then muster the patience to put that thought into layperson's terms and then make it digestible and usable for others to receive and understand it. This is one of Christian's unique abilities—and no doubt why this book will be so effective and practical in helping leaders implement an operating system to run world-class security teams.

This may be a burden of visionaries and thought leaders—an insatiable desire to innovate and make things better, a "never stop improving" attitude. In my prior life as an officer in the Army, I was taught to "never stop improving your fighting position." When is it done? The correct answer is that it's never done—something can always be done to improve it and make it better. Christian has taken this same approach in the service offerings and software that he has designed and implemented at risk3sixty.

Under Christian's leadership as CEO, we have never stopped at original methods, systems, or offerings—we have continuously improved over time by listening to clients, listening to our team, assessing industry needs and opportunities as they arise, and making decisions to improve our clients' and team's experiences. Since Christian has served as the firm's foremost thought leader and designer for our offerings, most notably in designing the Security Team Operating System, he is well-qualified to speak and write on this topic.

This book represents a progression of Christian's thoughts and activities over time. I view this as a masterclass on our most up-to-date and proven techniques and operating system, which we use internally and to help our clients build and manage great security teams and programs. For the newly initiated cybersecurity leader, studying and understanding the topics in this book will accelerate your understanding of how to operationalize and build a world-class security team and program. For the experienced security leader—for instance, the chief information security officer (CISO)—many concepts in this book will be familiar to you, but I expect that you have not yet seen an operating system so bespoke, simplified, and tied together for the infosec leader. For you, this book may serve to help you take your program to the next level.

My hope for you in reading this book is that you can quickly envision how to practically implement some or all of the Security Team Operation System in your organization. Beyond helping your team function as an elite security team, internalizing, and applying the concepts in this book will no doubt make you a more effective security and business leader, both in leading your team and in supporting your organization's goals and objectives.

Good luck!
C.F. White
President & Co-founder
Risk3sixty, LLC
Atlanta, Georgia

INTRODUCTION

The world has a shortage of leaders.

It always has.

Why? Because leadership requires a level of accountability most people are uncomfortable with. Leadership requires taking risks, patience, conflict, communication, moral courage, and a lot of other doggedly earned skills—skills most people resist.

Think about it. It takes courage to tell your team, "This is the strategy, here is the plan to execute the strategy, and I'm holding you all accountable to it." But that kind of clarity, courage, and conviction is exactly what people want from their leaders.

And, believe me, the people around you are begging for leadership. Even if you don't realize it. They want someone to paint a clear vision, to encourage them to set and hit goals, to manage conflict head-on, to establish an ethical standard, and to make hard decisions.

Leading people is a big job.

If you do it well, you can change the lives of the people under your leadership. If you do it really well, you can create new leaders who will go off and create the next generation of leaders. You will have the opportunity to watch people start families, buy homes, and sometimes change their lives. You can help people find meaning in their work.

What an amazing opportunity!

Great leaders define a clear purpose, establish a system of team values, define roles and responsibilities, get the team in an operational rhythm, and set and hit clear goals. Leaders take a group of random individuals and organize. They harness the potential energy of a team to accomplish a worthy mission. Every team needs someone to take on this responsibility. And that someone is *you.*

If you're reading this book, then you're ready to embrace the responsibility of leadership, but you aren't sure how to move forward. Your team feels stuck, sub-optimized, and lacking in clarity. You know there are better ways to lead a security team, but you aren't sure what they are.

It's not that you're ignorant or incompetent. It's just that leading a security team is much different from working as part of that team. Most security leaders reach their positions because they are skilled tacticians. But while those skills made you an excellent team member, they are not the same skills necessary to excel as a leader.

No one taught you how to lead. No one gave you the system.

I know from experience. I began as a cybersecurity practitioner and consultant before rising through the ranks into more leadership-oriented roles. At twenty-eight, I started a business, and then I became the CEO of that business. Quickly, I realized that while I could do the tactical part of that business well, I didn't know how to lead—and this lack of knowledge cost our business time, money, and good people.

Eventually, I realized that, in order to succeed, I needed to invest in myself as a leader. After working with hundreds of security professionals, I realized that other emerging security leaders need to do the same as well. Security leaders need a vision, a blueprint, and a system to help them run their team effectively.

I call this system the Security Team Operating System (STOS).

The Security Team Operating System is a proven process for information security leaders to run world-class security teams. The system described in this book is not theory. It is an operating system that I have used at my own company, that my department leaders have used, and that is in place at some of the best security organizations in the world. This system is the result of over 250 interviews with security leaders, assessing over one thousand security programs, firsthand experience working with great CEOs and military leaders, multiple studies on high-performing teams, and, most importantly, real-world experience.

This book is the distillation of that experience, taking the hard-earned lessons I've learned as a CEO and applying them to the context of running a security team. As of this writing, as the CEO of risk3sixty, I lead a team of over sixty people—roughly the size of the security team of a Fortune 500 company. That said, whether you lead a team of sixty or a team of five, the five-part operating system we will explore in this book works the same, enabling you to focus your attention and drive more clarity, better performance, and team culture.

The STOS is broken down into five essential components:

1. **Purpose:** Are you aligned with the business's most important objectives?

2. **Values:** How can you establish principles and values that build and enforce a strong team culture?

3. **Roles:** How can you set up your security team's organizational structure to support their team's objectives?

4. **Rhythms:** How can meeting agendas and cadences provide predictable and necessary structure to facilitate effective information sharing and communication?

5. **Goals:** How can leaders intentionally align the team's priorities to accomplish defined objectives?

You may already be familiar with some of these concepts. I did not invent them. In my experience, implementing the STOS both within my own organization and within large corporations, the value of this system is far greater than the sum of its parts. If you can get the five elements of this system working together in unison, you will have the makings of a *great* security team.

Security Isn't Just Systems and Processes

Creating a great security team is precisely why my partner C. F. White and I founded risk3sixty in the first place. We believed in the power of teams, and we believed in the power of working hard for something important. There is no greater feeling than being a part of a tight-knit team hell-bent on accomplishing great things.

And yet, for the first ten years of my career, I couldn't find that feeling anywhere. I changed jobs three times chasing it. At each stop, I felt like I was just going through the motions. Sure, I worked with good people, but we weren't united around a cause. Sixty-hour work weeks are a tough pill to swallow if you don't have a good reason for working so hard—and I didn't have a leader at the helm to provide a vision to believe in.

In the early years of my professional career, I was also coming off a ten-year run of participating in high school- and college-level sports. Some of the strongest teams and coaches I have ever been a part of set the bar high. I was used to working hard for the people on my team and for the coaches who set the tone from the top. I was looking for a *team* to build something great. But at my corporate jobs, no one told me *why* our work was important. So, I felt like it *wasn't* important—which made me feel absolutely miserable.

So, in 2016, my business partner and I launched risk3sixty. Finally with this new company, I was in a position to recreate that feeling of camaraderie I had been missing.

Only this time, my role was different: I wasn't a player anymore. I didn't have a coach or boss to tell me what to work for. *I* was the coach. *I* was the leader. It was my job as the CEO of a company to define what we did and why it mattered—and then to make sure that everyone on the team knew what that "important thing" was and bought in on it.

The more I focused on this problem, the more I realized that building a great team is much more about the *who* and the *why* than it is about the *what* and the *how*. To create that clarity for our team, we developed what we called the Management Operating System, which focused on the same five elements as the STOS outlined in this book: purpose, values, roles, rhythms, and goals.

The more we onboarded new team members into this system and the more we applied these principles to our work with other security teams, the more I realized that the Management Operating System could be applied more narrowly to help security teams find success. Set your teams up to succeed, give them something to believe in and work toward, and you will have the makings of a world-class security function.

The value of this operating system was clear—propelling risk3sixty to double in size every two years, reduce turnover, and become more adaptable to organizational growth and changes in the industry. But while the results and

want to help the organization accomplish its mission, you want to build a high-performing team, and you want to earn the respect of other executives. Here's how the STOS will help you accomplish that.

Better, Faster, More Confident Decision-Making

The number one job of a leader is to make ethical decisions in alignment with the company's core values—and quickly.

Remember what Theodore Roosevelt said: "In any moment of decision, the best thing you can do is the right thing, the next best thing is the wrong thing, and the worst thing you can do is nothing."

To make better decisions (that also let you sleep at night), leaders must have defined principles. They must also have a decision-making framework that ensures decisions are made in alignment with those principles.

Trust and credibility are built on a foundation of consistent adherence to an ethical code of conduct in alignment with core values. This is most important in difficult times when you have to disagree with people in a position of authority or go against the crowd. But when you can point to a clear purpose, values, roles, rhythms, and goals—it makes hard decision-making simple. There is incredible value in the ability to articulate to others how you arrived at a difficult decision.

That is the value of the STOS.

Clarity About Business Objectives

Security leaders should have absolute clarity about their business's greatest priorities. Often, this will include initiatives like new products, sales, large-scale implementations, entering new markets, and acquisitions. With this clarity, you can align your security team to initiatives that will support the organization as a whole. Clarity on business-level priorities will act as a sanity check to ensure your security program is focused on the right areas.

The added benefit is that this clarity will help you have more meaningful conversations with other executives. Asking for resources or pushing for organizational change becomes simpler when you have clarity about how your initiatives help move the business's goals forward.

Awareness of Other Business Priorities

As security leaders, we often place outsized priority on the initiatives we are passionate about. That is perfectly natural. It is a tough pill to swallow if security projects with a positive return on investment (ROI) are rejected. However, the reality is that business leaders allocate capital to dozens of projects. And some of those projects have a larger ROI than what we would like to accomplish in the cybersecurity domain.

That is where strong business acumen comes in.

By implementing the STOS, you will gain awareness of priorities and opportunities across the business. This knowledge will help you position security in the context of all of the potential opportunities that would benefit the business. In other words, it will help you more effectively pitch your project—or know when to back down if it is best for the business. As Sun Tzu said in *The Art of War*, "He will win who knows when to fight and when not to fight."

Socialize Ideas and Drive Change

Driving organizational change is a powerful skill. The best leaders I have worked with do an excellent job of getting collective buy-in and feedback on ideas before they officially make a request. This strategy helps get everyone on board, refines the idea, or crushes bad ideas in their infancy. It also demonstrates humility and a willingness to collaborate.

The STOS will provide techniques and opportunities to collaborate within your team and with leaders across the organization. As a result, you will gain a stronger intuition about what initiatives are important, more influence with decision-makers, and better tools to complete projects when given the opportunity.

Building a Great Team and Impacting Their Lives

The best leaders are judged by their team, not by their contributions. Great leaders provide a clear vision and have the tools to execute that vision consistently. But no leader can do it on their own. Leaders rely on their teams to carry out the mission. The STOS provides leaders with a system to build a great team with the capabilities to accomplish great things.

You will also enjoy the biggest gift of all: watching your team succeed. Your team members will become far more likely to enjoy their jobs, achieve their goals, and get the raises they want (and deserve). Some will buy homes, start families, and mature into high-performing professionals—and you will get to watch it all with pride as these essential contributors grow and flourish.

Let's Get Started

Now that you understand the basics of the STOS and how it will benefit both you and your team, you are probably anxious to start implementing this system and to see your team achieve all of these wonderful outcomes.

I am excited for you, I know you can do it, and I know the STOS can help you get there.

Before we get started, a few notes on what you can expect in the chapters that follow.

First, this book is not for individual contributors at a company. It's for people who are actively leading a security team. If you represent a security team of one and have little desire to manage or lead, this book is not for you.

Similarly, this is not a guide on how to get promoted to a security leadership role. You will not learn how to transition out of your analyst role into a management position. This book is for existing security leaders looking for a better system to lead their team.

Famous business coach Gino Wickman says in his book *Traction,* "You must have one abiding vision, one voice, one culture, and one operating system. This includes a uniform approach to how you meet, how you set priorities, how you plan and set your vision, the terminology you use, and the way you communicate to employees."[1]

---

[1] Gino Wickman. *Traction: Get a Grip on Your Business.* (BenBella Books: Dallas). 2012.

Gino is right.

Great security teams must be on the same page and rowing in the same direction. As a leader, if you can make this happen you will be able to achieve results you never believed possible.

Let's get started.

CHAPTER 1

WHAT YOU ARE ABOUT TO BUILD

Executive Summary

Have you ever read a business book and wished the author would have cut down the 150 pages into ten? Well, that is what I am doing in this chapter. This chapter is a twenty-minute overview of the entire Security Team Operating System (STOS) for busy executives. We will briefly cover each of the five elements of the STOS—Purpose, Values, Roles, Rhythms, and Goals. I will also list all of the downloadable resources available to you as part of this book. This chapter is to prepare you for the rest of this book and serve as a quick reference guide when you come back to revisit this material later. If you only read one chapter, make it this one.

Have you ever been punched in the face? I have.

It was in a small town in Eastern Tennessee. Johnson City, to be exact. It was at an ill-maintained sports complex where they were hosting a mixed martial arts (MMA) event. For the uninitiated, MMA is essentially cage fighting. And yes, I was on the ticket. It was my first-ever MMA event, and I was the first fight of the night.

How does one get involved in such an event? That is a fair question.

I was on the wrestling team at the University of Georgia. One of my team members joined an MMA gym. And after weeks of hearing stories about his extracurricular practices off-campus, I succumbed to peer pressure and decided to join him. Unsurprisingly, I loved it too.

A few months later, I found myself in Johnson City. Getting punched in the face. But why? That is another fair question.

With the benefit of hindsight, I have come to realize that the reason my team loved MMA and college wrestling was not because we were eager for a fight. In fact, it is quite the opposite—I have never been in a fight outside of sports. The real reason that my team members and I were drawn to the sport was something deeper.

Clarity of purpose.

My teammates were my best friends. We did hard things together. We trained. We watched each other improve. We went to tournaments. We celebrated each other's wins. And we were there for each other after each loss. There was a feeling of purpose and camaraderie that gave us a united cause and individual purpose.

Sports are like that, aren't they?

That's why so many people love them. They offer a clear vision and purpose, like a match to win, a trophy, or a championship. Sports have clear metrics to mark success or failure, like points, wins, and losses. Clear expectations like showing up to practice, making weight, and following the rules of the game. You receive immediate feedback on your progress. Built-in systems like these create absolute clarity and focus.

Then I entered the corporate world.

I was young, bright eyed, and naïve. I wanted the great team, I wanted the clear vision, I wanted to be part of a culture. I wanted to find my next purpose. Only, I joined a consulting company with about a hundred thousand employees.

It was a great company, and I had a good boss, but my experience was missing the fire that got me so excited to be a part of the teams I was accustomed to. For the most part, the day-to-day at my job lacked culture and was missing heart, and the work product lacked the pride of craftsmanship. I felt like I was going through the motions.

Reflecting on that job, I realize we were missing leadership. We were missing clarity. Without that leadership and clarity, we were distracted by about a hundred day-to-day tasks we thought were important—a project, a deliverable, a meeting, the next performance review, and so on.

What were we really working for? What were we building together? What does winning look like? Why didn't our boss tell us?

Does any of that sound familiar?

Are you doing the same thing to your team? Have you written down and communicated a clear vision? Does everyone understand your team's values? Do they understand their role and how to measure whether they are winning?

If not, that lack of clarity is diluting your team's focus, creating ambiguity, and hurting your team's performance. It's probably ruining your culture too.

If you're reading this, then I'm willing to bet the people on your team are begging for leadership. *Your* leadership. If you provide them with a little clarity, it will change everything. Clarity creates focus—and when a team can focus their energy on a clear mission, they can accomplish great things.

I hope that is what the Security Team Operating System (STOS) does for you and your team. The system I present in this book is designed to direct your focus on five elements that will have the biggest impact for your team: Purpose, Values, Roles, Rhythms, and Goals.

In this chapter, I will provide an overview of each of these elements so that you have a basic understanding of how the STOS works. If you prefer to learn by doing, this chapter should provide you with a basic understanding of the STOS so you can put this book down and build it on your own. In other words, consider this the summary of the entire book for busy executives. However, if you prefer to have a deeper understanding of how the STOS works before attempting to implement it yourself (including free tools and templates in each chapter), use this chapter as a primer to help you get the basic concepts under your belt before launching into the rest of the book.

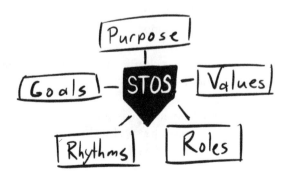

Purpose

> **Principle:** Leaders define a worthy mission and make it clear to their team.

If you polled your team and asked, "What is your purpose?," would every team member give the same answer? Probably not. With no clear purpose, teams tend to waste energy. A lot of it. They get pulled in different directions, gravitate toward shiny objects, and launch a temporary project out of every new idea.

You know a team like this when you see it. They often start out as high-energy or even chaotic. They have a hundred good ideas, but they see none of them through to completion. These characteristics are especially common among new team members—the bright-eyed rookies.

However, if these rookies never learn any better and a team of like-minded role players goes long enough without clarity, their energy and enthusiasm turns to cynicism and disenchantment. They start to feel like their ideas don't matter. They worry that their hard work will result in an unfinished project. Heck, they might even be punished for their efforts if they step out of line.

We have all seen the industry veteran who feels this way. Twenty years of experience. "It is, what it is," they say as they give you a knowing smile and take a sip of coffee.

You know the type, don't you?

It doesn't have to be this way. People want to do work that matters—both to the world and to themselves. Most people, especially high performers, aspire to do big things and to make a positive impact. If your team members feel like they are screw tighteners on an assembly line, they will quickly become disheartened and demotivated. When you define a clear focus, you help provide meaning and motivation to show up to work every day.

Jacob served in the Army as a Captain. He is about six feet tall, lean, stands up straight, looks you in the eyes when he speaks—he is exactly what you would expect out of an Army officer. After he left the Army, he came to work on my team as a cybersecurity consultant. One day over dinner, we discussed his transition from military service to the private sector.

"In the Army, I knew why I was there. I was there for a greater purpose. To try to do something good for my country and good for the people," he said. "In the private sector, it's less clear why we are here. To make money? To write the next report? That is a lot less motivating."

That conversation made a big impact on my perspective as a leader. Because I realized that one of the ways I could add value to my team was to help paint a clear picture of why we are here and what value we add. I could help rally our team around a common and meaningful mission.

- How do we serve society?
- How do we serve the goals of the company?
- How do we serve each other?

I feel so grateful to work in an industry that has such clear answers to questions like these. And as a leader, you have the opportunity to give your team the gift of clarity. You can harness the energy of the team around a clear and meaningful purpose. You can give your team the *why* behind the work they do.

And having a clear *why* will make a huge impact on your team.

Harvard and McKinsey & Company conducted an extensive study on a team's performance and satisfaction when it comes to tying the work we do to a clear purpose. Their results showed a clear correlation between purpose, performance, and satisfaction:

> Less satisfied [employees] reported lower average work and life outcomes than more satisfied peers did—everything from reduced feelings of energy and life satisfaction to lower engagement, satisfaction, and excitement about work. Negative work and life outcomes for employees inevitably translate to negative outcomes for the business.[2]

---

[2] Naina Dhingra, Andrew Samo, Bill Schaninger, and Matt Schrimper. "Help Your Employees Find Purpose—or Watch Them Leave." McKinsey & Company. April 5, 2021. https://www.mckinsey.com/capabilities/people-and-organizational-performance/our-insights/help-your-employees-find-purpose-or-watch-them-leave

Just over half (52 percent) of job seekers would not accept a job offer if they did not know or agree with a company's values or purpose. What's more, 90 percent of respondents from another poll said that work should bring a sense of meaning to their lives.[3]

As leaders, it is our responsibility to define our team's purpose. We must give our teams the *why* behind the *what*. This type of clarity will energize the team, rally them around a clear and defined objective, focus their efforts, and help ensure that their hard work results in positive outcomes for the business at large.

In Chapter 2: Purpose, we will provide a framework to:

1. Clearly identify and document the security team's purpose,
2. Ensure the security team's purpose is in harmony with clearly defined business objectives,
3. Understand the value of purpose statements and review examples from real security teams that you can draw inspiration from, and
4. Provide tools to ensure the defined purpose is communicated and understood by everyone on your team.

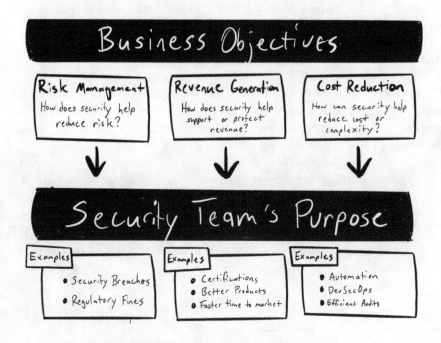

---

[3] Stephanie Santos. "Make Purpose Real for Employees." *Harvard Business Publishing*. September 30, 2022. https://www.harvardbusiness.org/make-purpose-real-for-employees/

Values

Principle: Defined values help a team act decisively and with confidence. Leaders establish principles and hold their team accountable to acceptable rules of behavior.

Many leaders are hesitant to have conversations with their team about core values. It can feel awkward and vulnerable to discuss the behaviors and principles that you care about, and it takes courage to put your feelings on the line and engage in an intimate conversation with colleagues. It can feel even more awkward to hold people accountable to your business's core values. However, formalizing your values will take your team's performance and camaraderie to the next level.

Teams that define and live by their values:

- Make better hiring decisions,
- Experience better employee performance and retention,
- Have higher employee satisfaction scores,
- Have a track record of making better and faster business decisions, and
- Hit their goals more consistently.

As a leader, you must have a set of principles that you have defined, that you believe in, and that you stand behind consistently. These principles will enable your team to set the standard, hold everyone accountable, and define the many intangible but essential elements of a high-performing team.

Lauren is the VP of Security for a global cloud infrastructure provider. She is charged with the operations of dozens of data center locations across the globe. At each location, she has a facilities manager responsible for the day-to-day management of the individual facility. Each facility manager has a team of around one hundred employees.

"We were having major consistency issues at some of our data center facilities. I was on phone calls for ten hours a day helping our facility manager navigate important decisions," Lauren said. "I was a major bottleneck for progress. I couldn't sleep at night, and I was seriously considering leaving the company."

The last straw came when an auditor sent her photos of one of her data center facilities. The facility was in awful condition. "There were wires all over the place. There was trash in one of the server cages. And there were several unlocked doors," Lauren said. "This was a huge surprise, and I couldn't believe it. I was so angry at myself and at the facility manager."

Lauren decided to have a meeting with her facility managers to determine the problem. So, she scheduled a team off-site meeting with all of her facility managers (see Chapter 5). During the meeting, they discovered that each member of the team had a very different set of standards for how they ran their respective facilities. "One facility manager described a hundred-point checklist to maintain data center cleanliness that the team completed each day. Another manager said he thought that it 'wasn't a big deal' how the data center looked on the inside as long as it hit its performance numbers," Lauren said.

Lauren decided they needed a defined set of expectations they would all buy into. During the meeting, Lauren grabbed a whiteboard and a marker and worked with the team to develop a set of core values that would become the standard for how they would run their facilities. They agreed to hold each other accountable to these values and discussed real-world examples of those values manifested in the workplace.

"One of the core values we developed was 'Right, for right's sake.' We agreed that it meant that all of our data centers would be as close to perfect as we could make them. We even started a group message where facility managers could share examples of their facility living by the core values," Lauren said. "I also noticed that I wasn't on the phone playing damage control as often. The conversation about our values and expectations gave our team what they needed to make decisions more autonomously. They didn't need to call me to get my opinion—they already knew what I would do. It was a huge, unexpected benefit."

Lauren later told me that she ultimately chose to fire one of her facility managers. Although he did work to define his team's values as asked, it was clear that he did not believe in them. Seeing this, Lauren decided he was not a good fit for the organization, and later hired another manager who has since become her top performer. As a result, her team is all on the same page about what they want to accomplish and the values they uphold.

Conversations about values are a forcing mechanism to discuss, formalize, and challenge each other on the behaviors the team is willing to accept in the workplace. Once everyone on the team understands and agrees to what is acceptable, it sets up the team to hold each other accountable. And when the team holds each other accountable, great things start to happen. Deadlines are met, goals are achieved, and a culture of excellence forms.

Values are a tool to help build a team that works well together. People who share a common sense of purpose agree on acceptable rules of behavior and are energized by the people they are surrounded by. As Jim Collins says in his famous book *Good to Great*, "If we get the right people on the bus, the right people in the right seats, and the wrong people off the bus, then we'll figure out how to take it someplace great."[4] Defined values are how your security team will build a team full of the right people who are energized about helping to accomplish important things.

In Chapter 3: Values, we will provide a framework to:

1. Identify and document your team's values,
2. Establish processes to integrate your core values into key business processes like hiring, performance reviews, and decision-making, and
3. Improve your team's culture by getting the right people on the team and the wrong people off the team.

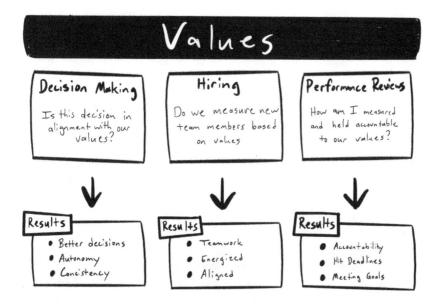

---

[4] Jim Collins. *Good to Great: Why Some Companies Make the Leap and Others Don't.* (New York: Harper Business), 2001.

Roles

Principle: Leaders ensure the right people are doing the right job to accomplish the mission.

Security teams are asked to do a lot. Often, roles and responsibilities are murky territory—expanding boundaries from vulnerability management to fielding compliance audits. There are literally dozens of jobs and hundreds of tasks. The sheer volume and diversity of responsibilities make security notoriously ambiguous and often overwhelming. This is one of the primary reasons why burnout is so prevalent on security teams.

Jordan is the chief information security officer (CISO) at a SaaS technology company that helps organizations process payments online. When Jordan first inherited the security program, he discovered that almost every element of the program was managed ad hoc. Every key function had unclear ownership, and key processes were inconsistent.

"I was very concerned when I first took over the security program. I would ask the team who owned a key function like vulnerability management or risk assessments, and I would get different answers," Jordan said. "I also noticed a pattern that three of my team members appeared to own the whole security program. Everyone else on the team looked to them for almost every key process. Those three people were extremely overworked. And if one of them left the company, I would be in big trouble."

Our team at risk3sixty worked with Jordan to reorganize the security team. We started by establishing an effective governance structure and then defining security program roles and responsibilities. The goal of the exercise was to define a security operating model that clarified all of the key functions, processes, and owners.

"The first thing we noticed is that our team was understaffed and didn't have the right skill set needed to support the security program. The second thing we noticed was that the team was very unclear about their roles and what was expected of them," Jordan said.

By defining and documenting the security program's roles and responsibilities, Jordan was able to work with the CFO to get additional resources for this team. Jordan was also able to work with his existing team to clearly define roles and key performance indicators for each role and to reduce the workload for some of the team members.

"When I accepted the job, the team had a lot of anxiety," Jordan said. "One of our team members called me crying one evening. She had too much on her plate and didn't want to let the team down. It was a very unhealthy place to be."

Since clarifying roles and hiring additional team members, Jordan's security team has become a new organization. "Now our team has one of the best cultures I have ever been a part of. I am proud of how far we have come," Jordan said.

Work doesn't have to be ambiguous. And it certainly doesn't have to be a source of anxiety.

Under your leadership, your team can have absolute clarity. You can give your team structure, you can define what success looks like for each role, and you can provide team-wide transparency. This type of clarity will energize the team and give them the clarity they need to do their job with quality. This simple step is liberating. It clears the mind to focus on the things that need to be done. With absolute clarity, you get focused energy and effort.

In Chapter 4: Roles, we will provide a framework to:

1. Understand and document your role as the team's leader,
2. Establish an effective security team governance structure,
3. Define the seven functions of a security team,
4. Define the roles and responsibilities across each of the seven functions, and
5. Leverage roles and responsibilities to identify gaps and inform your resource plans going forward.

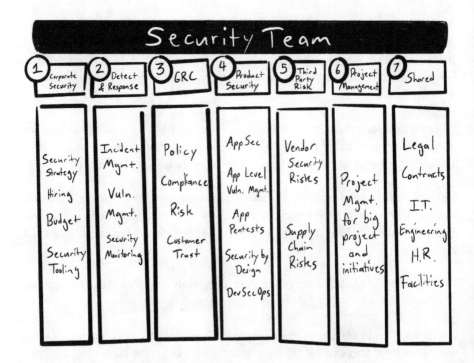

Rhythms

Principle: Leaders make sure everyone is on the same page.

Rhythms create flow. They create predictability for teams. The best teams use rhythms to ensure every team member has the right information at the right time on a predictable cadence. This reduces the need for ad hoc meetings and constant information gathering, and it creates an environment where every team member knows exactly what to expect.

Rhythms are the heartbeat of your team, and they are the mechanism by which we tie the entirety of the STOS together. The rhythms we discuss in this book will create the time and space for communication, information sharing, and culture building. Rhythms will make your entire team more efficient by creating a common language and getting everyone rowing in the same direction. Rhythms are one of the fastest ways to reduce chaos and create order.

John is the CISO at a large healthcare company that manages electronic healthcare records. A few years ago, the organization set a goal of implementing a governance, risk, and compliance (GRC) program to achieve certification for several security frameworks. To add to the complexity, the organization had recently acquired several businesses that they also needed to bring into the program and up to the company's standard.

John shared some of his experience:

> The first month on the project was total chaos. We had dozens of contacts across different departments and business units in the organization. There was no common understanding of goals, roles, and zero communication flow between key team members.
>
> We had two new acquisitions. I didn't know anyone on their team. The engineers refused to take calls from me. I couldn't ask them about policies, communicate with them about our certification goals, or even get to know them. It was a situation where no one knew what the other team was doing.

After a month, John had made very little progress. So, John decided to hold an all-hands meeting to begin the process of forging relationships and to develop a communication calendar.

"The calendar set up a cadence of annual, quarterly, and weekly rhythms. The rhythms created a common understanding of information flow, reduced ad hoc meetings, and created time and space for people to discuss critical issues," John said. "This single action got an otherwise disjointed organization on the same page."

A few months after achieving their security certifications, I received a call from John. He informed me that they had just landed the biggest healthcare system in the country as a new client. The client informed them that their security program's maturity was a big factor in choosing their company versus a competitor. John credits the rhythms the security team set up during the all-hands meeting as the turning point in the project—ultimately resulting in the project's success.

"The cadences we implemented to share information and get everyone on the same page have changed the trajectory of our security program. This year, we are doing our third annual security team off-site meeting, and there is a buzz in the office. Everyone is excited to see each other, give updates, and enjoy each other's company," John said. "Not only have these rhythms changed our team's performance, but it has also changed our culture."

Every security team needs a cadence of clear communication. This will help ensure that all team members have the right data, at the right time, to do their best work. In Chapter 5: Rhythms, will provide a framework to:

1. Build a one-page calendar of rhythms that will clarify team communication,
2. Establish a cadence of annual, quarterly, and weekly rituals with defined preparatory steps and desired outcomes, and
3. Document meeting agendas, data, and information that needs to be provided to the team, so they have what they need when they need it.

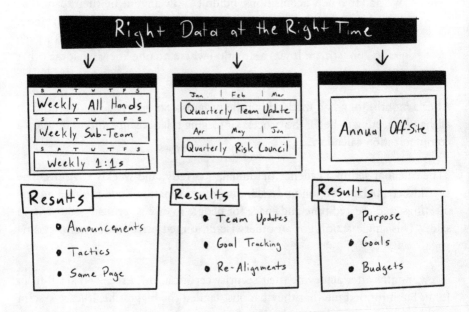

Goals

Principle: Leaders harness the team's energy to accomplish a clear objective.

As a leader, you have the opportunity to harness the energy of the team to accomplish your most important initiatives. You have the responsibility and opportunity to establish the objective and get everyone on the team working toward it. You can spark the team's energy and enthusiasm by making clear what you want to accomplish and helping people establish goals to accomplish it.

Goal setting is most powerful when the leader can rally the entire team around a single objective. Often, team members will set great goals, but the goals are often ad hoc and chosen on a member-by-member basis. The result is a jumble of disjointed efforts that fail to help the security team accomplish its most important team objectives. To practice goal setting successfully,

1. Understand the company's biggest objectives.
2. Align the security team's objectives to the company's objectives.
3. Set team level goals to help accomplish the security team's objectives.
4. Set individual goals to help accomplish the team's objectives.

The best security leaders get these four priorities right.

Phil is a renowned CISO known for being a people-focused leader. When he earned his first leadership opportunity, he knew he wanted to focus on helping his team develop personally and professionally. Said Phil:

> I wanted to see our team do great things. I asked every team member to document goals that would help them get to the next level personally and professionally. I dedicated budgets for training, events, and coaching. Our team members created dozens of goals. One team member received leadership training, another team member received a certification for graphic design, and we had other team members set goals to spend more time with family. I was energized to see the team set and achieve their goals.

Phil may have been energized to watch his team meet personal goals, but their goal setting initiative came with unintended consequences: the team missed their objective for the year and missed out on an important bonus opportunity.

"At the end of the year, I realized that everyone set great goals, but almost none of the goals focused our team's energy on the business's objective," Phil said. "Instead, I let our team get distracted by fun ideas that ultimately did not impact our objective. "My heart was in the right place, but the execution wasn't there."

The following year, Phil reset his goal setting methodology. Instead, he provided clear business and security team objectives that the team had to align their individual goals. Phil also implemented a system where managers could challenge and support team members to create clearer and more actionable goals. Each team member also had to be specific about how each goal would support the security team's objective.

"After we realigned our goal setting formula, it changed everything. Not only did people accomplish personal goals, but we also exceeded every business objective," Phil said. "What surprised me most was how much it energized the team. We were twice as energized working toward a common goal than the year before when everyone set unrelated, individualized goals."

In Chapter 6: Goals, we will provide a framework to:

1. Define and communicate a clear team objective,
2. Establish individual goals that helps accomplish the team's objective, and
3. Develop a system of tracking and accountability to help ensure everyone accomplishes their goals.

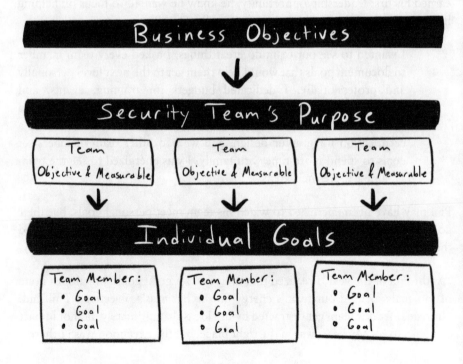

It's Time to Change the Way You Lead

From here, we are going to use the rest of the book to do a deep dive into each of the five areas of the Security Team Operating System.

As we dive in, remember one thing: this system will change the way you lead.

How do I know? Because that's what it did for me—and for the hundreds of other security leaders who have implemented it as well.

When I first launched risk3sixty as a young entrepreneur, I placed a lot of value on being an expert. But as my team grew, I realized I was underserving my team. My team didn't need an expert. It needed a leader. Without a system, our company's health and culture suffered. We lost good people and wasted energy, and I worked too many eighty-hour weeks, lost too much sleep, and waited too long to delegate tasks so I could focus on being the leader my team needed me to be. I undervalued things that I now understand to be essential.

But then our team decided to implement this system.

We got serious about our purpose, values, roles, rhythms, and goals. And when we did, it unlocked a new level of potential. For me personally, the system paved the way for me to become a more effective leader both at work and at home. I was able to set a vision for my team and get out of their way.

By following the STOS, we unlocked a new level of performance for our business. We started attracting top talent and clients. We earned awards, like *Consulting Magazine's* "Best Firms to Work For" and placement on the Fastest Growing Companies list for the last six years and counting.

Most importantly, we created great opportunities for everyone inside the company. I've watched people start families, buy homes, send their kids to college, and support their aging parents. And as for me, I was able to focus my energy on other important things—like spending time with my family and writing this book.

Man, that is the good stuff.

I credit much of our success to our operating system, which created focus and harmony within our organization and harnessed the energy of our team to accomplish important things—and the results have been amazing.

I hope this book enables you to unlock new potential for yourself and your team like I have seen it impact so many others.

Download the Tools

For the rest of the book, at the end of each chapter, I will provide a list of tools and next steps to help you put these concepts into practice. These tools will include free downloads from our website, recommended reading, and other useful resources.

To access these resources, please visit: https://risk3sixty.com/stos

CHAPTER 2

PURPOSE

Executive Summary

Leaders make clear a worthy mission. In this chapter, we will discuss how leaders can identify their security team's purpose and how to ensure that purpose aligns with the business's most important objectives. Once you feel confident in your team's purpose, we will then cover examples and provide tools to help you ensure your entire team is clear about what needs to happen and why it is important.

Self-Assessment Questions

☐	What are the key objectives for your company this year?
☐	What are the key objectives for your security team this year? Are the objectives of your security team clearly mapped to the objectives of the company?
☐	Are your security team's objectives documented and shared with the team?
☐	Could each member of your team recite the objectives of your company and the objectives of your security team?

Why do we do the things we do?

Out of habit? Because someone told us we have to? Because we saw someone else do it, so we followed suit?

We show up to work, we log in to our computer, check our email, and browse the internet—old habits performed almost on autopilot.

This is a waste of life. And it's depressing.

Thankfully, it's also avoidable. To create a more meaningful life and to create a more meaningful experience at work, start by asking yourself and your team an important question: What is your purpose?

Stacy was on a project leading a team of fifty engineers and business analysts to create a vulnerability management integration across four business units' IT infrastructure. Her challenge: each of the four business units operated independently. Stacy had to work with four different product leaders, and she couldn't get them to work together.

"Honestly, we were failing," Stacy said. "The product was becoming bloated, every integration had bugs, and there were a dozen half-finished features. The business units would not allocate engineering time to let us test the product. It was very frustrating to our security team and demoralizing to the engineers. Our CIO told me he thought we were probably wasting our time."

After three months, in a gambit to create clarity for both her and her team, Stacy organized a meeting between the chief information officer (CIO), IT leaders, and security leadership across each business unit. Immediately, Stacy kicked off the meeting by grabbing a white board and asking a series questions:

- What problem(s) are we trying to solve?
- What would be the ideal future if this problem was solved?
- How does this save us time and money?
- How does this make our security better?
- How does this support the business's objectives?

The answers were all over the place. "Everyone had a different agenda or a different goal in mind," Stacy said. Undeterred, Stacey focused on being a good listener and asking good questions.

It worked. After a two-hour working session, the entire team was aligned on a single, clear purpose. As the discussions revealed, this project was vital to the company's success in several ways. Successful execution of this project would:

- Save the company at least $10 million a year.
- Rescue their relationship with a major customer with a contract value of $5 million per year, who had demanded major improvements in their infrastructure security.
- Improve retention for a vulnerability management team whose members were burning out and leaving every twelve months.

With everyone on the same page and clear on why this project was mission-critical to the organization, each leader committed to supporting Stacy going forward.

But Stacy didn't stop there. Next, she created a purpose statement and shared it with the entire team. "I made a sign and hung it in our office, I made it front and center on our internal team website, and we integrated it into our weekly status report," Stacy said. "Understanding how this helped the business was a big motivator for everyone."

This "big motivator," as Stacy put it, might have made the difference between a failing project and a resounding success. Stacy's efforts showed real leadership.

The result was not only a big win for her company, but also for Stacy herself. At the company's annual meeting later that year, Stacy was given an award for her work on the project. Two years later, she was promoted to CISO of the organization, a role she held for the next six years. As of this writing, she is now the organization's corporate CIO. And she can trace all her success to the moment she decided to take the power of purpose seriously.

By aligning your team's purpose statement with your business's objectives, you can provide your team with a clear direction and focus. This clarity can help to ensure that your team's efforts are focused on the most important tasks and activities that will drive the business forward. In this chapter, you'll learn how to create a compelling purpose statement to align your team and produce powerful results.

Why Purpose Matters

There are two reasons you need to take the process of defining your purpose seriously:

1. Your team's sense of purpose
2. Your ability to support the business's objectives

In the following sections, we'll explore each of these ideas.

Your Team's Sense of Purpose

Most folks are amazed to see how a clear purpose can change a team's culture. But the fact remains: a clear purpose can fire up a team, giving them the strength to accomplish important missions and work together to accomplish big goals. With a good enough reason to fight for a cause, a good purpose can even turn the deepest cynics into the staunchest champions.

In other words, doing stuff that matters is all that matters. And as a leader, *it is your job* to make sure your team knows why what they do matters.

According to renowned business coach Dan Sullivan, teams need inspirational motivation. To achieve this, leaders must "articulate a vision that is appealing and inspiring to your team." Sullivan continues:

> You challenge your team to increase their personal standards, while you communicate optimism about future goals, and provide meaning for the task at hand. . . . As the visionary and leader, your ability to powerfully and persuasively communicate the vision is essential. You must make the vision understandable, precise, powerful, and engaging so that your team will become increasingly willing to put more effort into completing their tasks.[5]

Coming up with the kind of *why* that will unite your team is hard work. It is the type of work most of us aren't used to: thought work.

---

[5] Dan Sullivan and Dr. Benjamin Hardy. *Who Not How.* (California: Hays House Business, 2020).

But it has to be done. A team's purpose can only come from the leader. It is up to the leader to do the deep thinking, put pen to paper, and be bold enough to paint a vision for the team. No one else is going to do this work for you.

Your Ability to Support the Business's Objectives

In addition to firing up your team, your team's purpose must also get everyone running in the right direction to support the business. Otherwise, your team is wasting its time—and the company's.

That's one of the big challenges for cybersecurity leaders.

As I said in the introduction, we are an industry full of technical experts, hackers, contrarians, anarchists, and anti-authoritarians. We are used to thinking about the bad stuff that could happen. We think about the risks. We think about how problems will be solved.

What we do not spend enough time thinking about is why the business needs us to solve these problems in the first place. What is the business driver? Why is the business willing to make the investment? Without focusing on these questions, security leaders can get out of touch with the business they work for.

Often, this kind of misalignment with the business can create a dangerous cynicism—even negativity. I see it at conferences, in conversations with other security leaders, and among friends. Sometimes there is a feeling that the business and the security operation are at odds. That the business is not listening or doesn't care. That they pay lip service to security but aren't willing to dedicate the resources to actually solve the problems.

But I don't think that's true.

The business and the security team are on the same larger team, even if we sometimes have trouble seeing things the same way. Either the security leader is missing the big picture or the business hasn't been clear about its objectives. Maybe both.

Great security leaders can solve this challenge. They can harmonize the needs of the business with the capabilities of the security team. They can identify the needs of the business. They can examine how security can help play a big role in those objectives. They can influence the right people. They can listen more.

They can do the work of understanding why they exist. They can be the great translator between business objectives to security team objectives. Then they can get the security team energized around a clear and important mission.

That's purpose!

Thinking Model: 3 Ways Security Supports Business Objectives

If you are struggling to map your security team's purpose back to the organization's broader objectives, here is a secret: there are only three reasons a business relies on its security team.

1. Risk management
2. Revenue generation
3. Cost containment

Use these three business objectives as a shortcut to create your security team's purpose statement and map it back to the organization's overall objectives. For the rest of the chapter, I'll describe each of the primary business objectives, explore ways you can get a better understanding of those objectives, and review a few real-world examples of purpose statements.

Business Objective #1: Risk Management

Every organization wants to manage risk. For most security professionals, this objective is also the most intuitive. If you ask most security professionals why they do what they do, they will tell you it is because they want to protect both their company's and their customers' data.

And they are right.

One of our clients at risk3sixty runs a cloud platform that manages electronic health records for several major healthcare systems. The platform has an internet-facing website where patients can log in to access their data. Our team was asked to perform penetration testing on this web portal as part of a security check. On the first day of the engagement, our team was able to exfiltrate patient records directly from the internet-facing web portal using a very common attack method called SQL injection.

This platform has been on the market for over a decade and houses hundreds of thousands of patient records. Had a malicious actor exploited this vulnerability, it would have had disastrous consequences for the organization and its patients. To complicate the situation further, the organization was also in the process of completing two major acquisitions. A breach of this magnitude would have put those business deals at risk. Luckily, the organization was able to perform a simple system upgrade to resolve the issue.

Our team has found hundreds of similar issues at other organizations. Cyber risks are very real and can have a monumental impact on businesses. Companies need security professionals to watch their backs and anticipate the myriad ways their systems and data could be attacked. This is important work that has to be done. The board of directors, executives, and customers care about keeping their company safe—just like their security teams.

Creating Purpose Statements for Risk Management Objectives

Here are a few examples you can use as inspiration to incorporate in your purpose statement for risk management:

- **Developing a cybersecurity maturity roadmap:** By creating a comprehensive cybersecurity maturity roadmap, we align our security initiatives with our business objectives and risk management strategy. This roadmap outlines the necessary steps and milestones to enhance our cybersecurity capabilities, accounting for our current security posture, industry best practices, and emerging threats.

- **Prevent a security breach:** By implementing robust cybersecurity measures, we mitigate the risk of unauthorized access to sensitive data, safeguarding our customers' and stakeholders' confidential information.

- **Safeguarding reputation:** Cybersecurity measures protect our organization's reputation by preventing security breaches that could lead to negative publicity, loss of trust from customers and stakeholders, and damage to our brand image.

- **Preventing financial loss:** Effective cybersecurity practices help us prevent financial losses resulting from data breaches, cyberattacks, and other security incidents, thereby ensuring the financial stability and sustainability of our organization.

- **Ensuring business continuity:** By mitigating the risk of cyber threats, we minimize the potential disruptions to our business operations, maintaining continuity even in the face of potential cyber incidents.

- **Ensuring compliance:** Robust cybersecurity controls help us meet regulatory requirements and industry standards, reducing the risk of noncompliance penalties, legal consequences, and reputational damage.

- **Minimizing legal liabilities:** By implementing effective cybersecurity practices, we reduce the risk of legal liabilities resulting from data breaches, ensuring compliance with data protection and privacy laws.

- **Protecting intellectual property:** Cybersecurity measures safeguard our intellectual property, preventing unauthorized access, theft, or compromise of proprietary information, trade secrets, and research and development data.

- **Managing third-party risks:** As we collaborate with various third-party vendors, partners, and service providers, cybersecurity helps us manage the associated risks. By conducting thorough cybersecurity assessments, due diligence, and ongoing monitoring, we mitigate the risk of data breaches or security incidents originating from third-party relationships, protecting our organization and its stakeholders from potential financial, legal, or reputational harm.

While risk management is an essential function of cybersecurity teams, it is not the only area security teams can add business value. Security teams can also contribute with revenue generating activities and support sales.

For more examples, please visit: https://risk3sixty.com/stos

Business Objective #2: Support Revenue by Earning Customer Trust

Every organization must sell their products and services to make money. And almost every organization has corporate goals to grow revenue and retain clients. Cybersecurity directly supports both of these goals.

How?

Have you ever been asked to complete a security questionnaire? Do you have contracts that require security certifications or commitments related to cybersecurity? Does your organization have a reputation to maintain in the marketplace?

These types of requirements are becoming table stakes for doing business. And for many organizations, the ability to explain their cybersecurity program is an essential step to sell products and services to their customers. So, if your business objective is focused on growth, selling, and retaining revenue—your team should be focused on this as well.

Here are a few examples:

Security Certifications

If your security team supports security certifications, it is probably because your customers require it. It means that your security team directly supports the company's ability to protect existing revenue and acquire new sales from clients.

Why are security certifications so common?

We live in a digital economy. Every company relies on other companies to do business. We outsource key business processes and share data. There are software-as-a-service (SaaS) companies for everything. There are even SaaS companies to manage your SaaS companies.

And this is a good thing.

The explosion of digital partnerships has resulted in huge efficiencies and innovation. Cloud computing, automated processes, artificial intelligence, virtual storefronts, and cryptocurrency all enable new ways to collaborate and improve the ability to work from anywhere. Because of this, companies can focus on their core competencies instead of administrative tasks. Leaders can think about strategy and automate repeatable tasks. My kids can ask my alarm clock for a joke. The digital economy has ushered in a new era, and I am grateful to be here for it.

But there are important risks too.

- According to a survey by Ponemon Institute, 59 percent of organizations have experienced a data breach caused by a third-party vendor or contractor.[6]
- The average organization has 583 third-party vendors with access to their networks or data.[7] Gartner found that 60 percent of organizations work with as many as 1,000 third-party vendors.[8]
- In 2023, the average cost of a data breach involving a third-party vendor was $4.45 million, up from $3.86 million in 2020.[9]

The result: An endless slew of cybersecurity and privacy certifications: SOC 1, SOC 2, SOC 3, ISO 27001, ISO 27701, ISO 22301, NIST 800–171, NIST 800–53, CMMC, FedRAMP, HIPAA, HITRUST, PCI DSS, Cloud Security Alliance,

---

[6] Opus & Ponemon Institute. "Opus & Ponemon Institute Announce Results of 2018 Third-Party Data Risk Study: 59 Percent of Companies Experienced a Third-Party Data Breach, Yet Only 16 Percent Say They Effectively Mitigate Third-Party Risks." *Business Wire*. November 15, 2018. https://www.businesswire.com/news/home/20181115005665/en/Opus-Ponemon-Institute-Announce-Results-of-2018-Third-Party-Data-Risk-Study-59-of-Companies-Experienced-a-Third-Party-Data-Breach-Yet-Only-16-Say-They-Effectively-Mitigate-Third-Party-Risks
[7] Ibid.
[8] Gartner. "Third-Party Risk Management (TPRM)." Accessed Feb. 26, 2024. https://www.gartner.com/en/legal-compliance/insights/third-party-risk-management
[9] IBM. *Cost of Data Breach Report 2023.* July 24, 2023. https://www.ibm.com/reports/data-breach

customer audits, vendor questionnaires, contractual terms, and the list of requirements go on.

These certifications are driven by a need for visibility and assurance. Customers and prospects need to trust their business partners. And security teams are being asked to play an important role in helping to get certifications, sit in on sales calls, answer security questions from clients, and otherwise support an organization's need to earn the trust of their customers.

New Markets and New Products

Your organization probably aspires to do business with larger companies and land bigger contracts. But these larger organizations will require more from your organization to do business. They will probably require more insurance, more customer support, more contractual obligations for cybersecurity. That's where you come in. A mature cybersecurity program may help your organization do business with bigger, more complex, and more regulated prospects—and earn bigger contracts worth more money.

In heavily regulated industries, such as healthcare, finance, and government, cybersecurity is a critical concern for customers. These customers have high standards for security and compliance and often require their vendors and partners to have mature cybersecurity programs and relevant certifications to ensure the protection of their sensitive information.

Do you know who your current customers are? Do you know which industries or types of companies your organization aspires to do business with? By tracking down answers to questions like these, you would have the necessary information to prepare a purpose statement and security strategy that explicitly supports your organization in earning the trust of important healthcare clients, for instance. Winning sales opportunities for great companies is a worthy mission that your security team will be proud to support.

Creating Purpose Statements for Revenue Generation and Customer Trust Objectives

Here are a few examples you can use as inspiration to incorporate into your purpose statement for revenue generation and customer trust:

- **Demonstrating compliance:** Robust cybersecurity practices help us comply with data protection and privacy regulations, industry standards, and customer expectations. Demonstrating compliance not only avoids potential penalties but also enhances customer trust in our commitment to protecting their data, leading to increased revenue opportunities.

- **Enabling secure product innovation:** By integrating cybersecurity into the development and deployment of new products or services, we ensure their security and resilience. This allows us to introduce innovative offerings to the market with confidence, attracting new customers and generating additional revenue streams.

- **Enhancing brand reputation:** A strong cybersecurity posture positively influences our brand reputation. By proactively protecting customer data and preventing security incidents, we differentiate ourselves from competitors, build trust, and attract more customers, leading to increased revenue opportunities.

- **Security as a competitive advantage:** By establishing a reputation for strong cybersecurity practices, we differentiate ourselves from competitors and gain a competitive edge. This attracts customers who prioritize security, leading to increased revenue and market share.

- **Accelerating product development and release:** By incorporating cybersecurity considerations into the product development lifecycle from the beginning, we ensure that security is built into our products and services from the outset. This proactive approach enables us to address potential security vulnerabilities early on, reducing the need for post-release patches or updates.

As a result, we can bring new products and features to market faster, gaining a competitive advantage and generating revenue sooner while maintaining the necessary security controls.

- **Providing transparent security measures:** By being transparent about our cybersecurity practices, we instill confidence in our customers and demonstrate our commitment to protecting their data and privacy. We openly communicate the security measures we have in place, such as encryption protocols, access controls, and regular security audits. This transparency builds trust and gives customers the assurance that their information is safeguarded, leading to increased customer satisfaction, loyalty, and ultimately revenue growth.

- **Streamlining customer security assessments:** By establishing robust cybersecurity practices, we can efficiently complete customer security questionnaires and inquiries. We have comprehensive documentation and information readily available regarding our security controls, data protection measures, incident response plans, and compliance frameworks. This allows us to respond promptly and accurately to customer inquiries, providing the necessary information to address their security concerns.

Business Objective #3: Cost and Complexity Reduction

Great security teams are also great simplifiers. They help the business navigate a complex web of technical challenges, emerging threats, industry jargon, compliance certifications, and government regulations. And for many organizations, an aligned security team can offer an incredible amount of value by helping to reduce the cost and complexity of the organization's cybersecurity program.

According to Josh Wilckison, the Head of Security and Privacy at a global technology company, security and compliance requirements can cost a company millions of dollars each year. "Worse," Josh said, "compliance can take precious time from our engineering team and slow down our product development efforts. If I let it get out of hand, fielding audits can even erode the great culture we have built."

To address this concern, Josh rallied his security team around a cost and complexity reduction mission—and it made a huge difference for the organization.

Imagine the power of telling your team something like the following:

> We are going to eliminate the burden of compliance audits forever so our engineering team can focus on software. We are going to help our engineers automate vulnerability management so they can focus on building the greatest products we've ever produced. We are going to save the company $1 million this year. We are going to preserve our culture.

Would that be a worthwhile objective? Is that something that your team could get behind? Is that an objective other executives would support?

Absolutely.

Creating Purpose Statements for Cost and Complexity Reduction Objectives

Here are a few examples you can use as inspiration to incorporate in your purpose statement for cost and complexity reduction:

- **Simplifying compliance efforts**: Strong cybersecurity practices facilitate compliance with data protection regulations and industry standards. By proactively addressing security requirements, we reduce the complexity and costs associated with achieving and maintaining compliance, avoiding penalties and potential business disruptions.

- **Rationalizing technology investments**: Our team will spend money wisely, solve clear problems, and avoid tool duplication. We will also consider security requirements and potential risks at the beginning of the requirements-gathering phase, which will help avoid retrofitting security controls later.

- **Reducing insurance premiums:** Demonstrating a robust cybersecurity posture can lead to reduced insurance premiums. Insurers often provide incentives and discounts for organizations with effective cybersecurity measures in place, reflecting the lower risk profile and potential for fewer claims.

- **Simplifying security awareness and education:** By making cybersecurity concepts and best practices easy to understand and digestible for employees, we promote a culture of security within the organization. This includes providing clear and concise guidelines, training materials, and resources that help employees grasp key security principles and apply them in their daily work routines.

- **Seamless integration of security tools and processes:** By selecting and implementing user-friendly security tools and processes, we simplify the integration of security into employees' daily work routines. This includes leveraging automation, intuitive interfaces, and streamlined workflows that reduce complexity and minimize the effort required to adhere to security protocols.

- **Streamlined compliance audits:** By establishing robust cybersecurity practices and maintaining comprehensive documentation, we simplify the process of external audits for regulatory compliance. We proactively organize and present necessary evidence, such as security controls, risk assessments, policies, and incident response plans, in a structured and easily accessible manner.

- **Clear and practical security policies:** By developing security policies that are written in plain language and tailored to our organization's specific business requirements and processes, we ensure that employees can easily understand and follow them. These policies are designed to align with our unique operational needs, accounting for factors such as industry regulations, customer expectations, and technological capabilities.

Three Ways to Uncover Business Objectives

If you are a security leader tasked with safeguarding your company's assets and information, you may find yourself pondering a fundamental question: How the heck do you track down what your company truly cares about? In the complex landscape of business operations, it can be challenging to identify the all-important business objectives that drive decision-making and shape the direction of your organization.

It can be even more challenging for your team if you don't. We once worked with a company whose engineering and cloud teams spent months designing and building a new tool for the healthcare industry. Unfortunately, the teams weren't informed that this new product was meant for healthcare, so it lacked the much more stringent security features and certifications necessary for that industry.

During a strategy meeting a month before the product's release, the chief technology officer (CTO) and chief revenue officer (CRO) realized the gap. With no other choice, the team had to postpone the project timeline by six months. This oversight cost the company millions of dollars in labor and lost opportunities—all because the business objectives were unclear across the organization.

If you want to avoid a situation like this, get in tune with what your business wants to accomplish and prioritize your security team's objectives accordingly. As the team leader, it is up to you to do the hard work of understanding exactly what the company cares about, the goals they have set, and how you can mobilize your team to accomplish them.

But how do you uncover business objectives like these?

The following three approaches should help. And don't worry. It's okay if you don't memorize all the details right now. I recommend flagging this page for reference during your annual risk assessment and planning process meetings so you can explore each potential avenue one by one.

#1: Read Company Reports

You can learn a lot about your company by reading the official and unofficial documentation produced by company leadership and other departments.

Reading information such as annual reports, strategic presentations, risk registers, prior security reports, and budgets will provide you with the perspectives and historical context in which your organization operates. Reading is a shortcut to understanding what is important to your business.

Annual Reports

An annual report is a comprehensive document that publicly traded companies are required to file with regulatory bodies such as the Securities and Exchange Commission (SEC) in the United States, and which outlines the company's financial performance, business operations, and future plans.

Annual reports provide detailed information about a company's operations, including its financial performance, market position, and strategic plans. By reviewing the report, you can gain insight into a company's objectives, strategies, and potential risks.

For example, the report may provide information on the company's investments in research and development, which could signal a commitment to growth in a certain market segment. Similarly, the report may detail the company's supply chain, revealing potential vulnerabilities to supply chain disruptions or security breaches.

Strategic Presentations

Every company produces internal strategy presentations to communicate their business strategies, goals, and plans to employees. These presentations can be a valuable source of information for understanding the business's objectives and how they may impact your role in cybersecurity.

Here are a few ways in which internal strategy presentations can be useful:

1. **Understanding the company's overall vision:** Insight into the company's overall vision, mission, and values.

2. **Identifying departmental goals**: Goals and objectives for specific departments or teams.

3. **Learning about upcoming initiatives**: Upcoming initiatives or projects that are in the pipeline. By understanding these initiatives, you can prepare for any changes that may be coming and identify opportunities to contribute to their success.

4. **Understanding key metrics:** Internal strategy presentations may also provide information about key metrics that the company is tracking to measure its progress toward its objectives. By understanding these metrics, you can better understand how your work contributes to the company's success and identify opportunities for improvement.

Product Roadmaps

As the security leader, you must be aware of what your company is building and who they are building it for. Reviewing the company's product roadmap can be highly beneficial for cybersecurity strategic planning. Here are several ways in which it can help you prepare:

1. **Identify upcoming security features:** By examining the product roadmap, you can gain insights into the new security features and enhancements planned for implementation. This knowledge allows you to align your strategic planning with the evolving capabilities of the product. You can anticipate how these features may impact your cybersecurity strategy and plan.

2. **Plan for integration and compatibility:** Reviewing the product roadmap helps you anticipate future updates and releases. This knowledge enables you to integrate new versions of the product into your cybersecurity infrastructure. You can assess the compatibility of upcoming changes with your existing security measures, identify potential integration challenges, and plan for any necessary adjustments or updates.

3. **Enhance collaboration with product teams:** Product roadmaps offer key insights into the future direction of a product. This knowledge can foster collaboration with the product development teams, enabling you to provide feedback, suggest security enhancements, and actively participate in shaping the product's security features. Building strong relationships with the product teams enhances the alignment between

cybersecurity and product development, leading to better security outcomes.

4. **New customer use cases:** Working closely with the product team will help you proactively identify new or emerging use cases for your products (e.g., collecting new types of data, collecting payments, or serving new customer types). This knowledge will help you proactively identify new regulatory and compliance factors and predict emerging customer expectations.

Sales and Marketing Plans

Another way to understand what your company is focusing on is by reviewing sales and marketing plans. These plans will provide insight into the products and services your company is selling, and which markets your company plans to serve. Here's how it can help you prepare:

1. **Identify target markets and customer segments:** Sales and marketing plans often outline the target markets and customer segments the organization intends to focus on. By reviewing these plans, you can identify the specific industries, sectors, or customer types the organization aims to serve. This information helps you align your cybersecurity strategy to address the unique security challenges and requirements of those target markets.

2. **Understand customer needs and pain points:** Sales and marketing plans provide valuable information about customer needs and pain points. By examining these plans, you can gain insights into the cybersecurity challenges customers are facing or anticipate in the future. Understanding these pain points allows you to tailor your strategic planning to address those specific security needs effectively.

3. **Align security messaging and positioning:** Sales and marketing plans outline the messaging and positioning strategies to promote the organization's products or services. By reviewing these plans, you can align your cybersecurity strategy with the messaging and positioning of the organization. This alignment ensures that the security measures and solutions you develop are in line with the overall value proposition communicated to customers, enhancing the organization's brand and competitive advantage.

4. **Identify market trends and competitive landscape:** Sales and marketing plans often include market analysis and competitor research. By examining these plans, you can gain insights into emerging market trends, evolving customer expectations, and the competitive landscape. This knowledge allows you to adapt your cybersecurity strategy to address new threats, leverage market opportunities, and differentiate yourself from competitors.

5. **Plan for marketing and awareness campaigns:** Sales and marketing plans include details about upcoming marketing and awareness campaigns. By reviewing these plans, you can anticipate the messaging and themes that will be used to educate customers about the organization's products or services. This knowledge enables you to align your cybersecurity strategy with marketing initiatives, ensuring that your security measures and value propositions are effectively communicated to customers.

Prior Security Assessments

Reading prior cybersecurity assessments can be an important first step in strategic planning for your cybersecurity team. These assessments can provide insight into the current state of the organization's cybersecurity posture, identify potential vulnerabilities and risks, and highlight areas where improvements are needed.

Here are a few ways in which reading prior cybersecurity assessments can be useful:

1. **Understanding the current state of cybersecurity:** Prior cybersecurity assessments can provide a detailed analysis of the organization's current cybersecurity posture, including its strengths and weaknesses. By understanding the current state of cybersecurity, you can better identify the gaps that need to be addressed and prioritize your efforts accordingly.

2. **Identifying potential vulnerabilities and risks:** Cybersecurity assessments often identify potential vulnerabilities and risks within the organization's IT systems and infrastructure. By reviewing these assessments, you can identify areas that may be particularly vulnerable to attack and take steps to mitigate these risks.

3. **Highlighting areas for improvement:** Prior cybersecurity assessments can also highlight areas where the organization's cybersecurity posture needs improvement.

4. **What has been tried before:** Prior cybersecurity assessments can provide some insight into where the organization is coming from. For example, what initiatives have gone well and where has the organization historically struggled. This type of historical context will help arm you with information to better navigate future initiatives.

Prior Team Performance Reviews

If you want to earn the trust of your team, take an interest in their growth. From a strategic planning perspective, reviewing your team members' prior performance reviews provides valuable insights into your team members' strengths and weaknesses, as well as the priorities and effectiveness of your team as a whole.

Here are two areas to consider:

1. **Identifying areas of interest and expertise:** Performance reviews may also highlight areas where team members have a particular interest or expertise. By understanding these areas, you can better staff them on projects and work that align team members' roles and responsibilities with their interests and skills.

2. **Prior goals and individual time management:** As a leader, it is helpful to understand how your team members are spending their time. Do their goals align to objectives that help move the security team and business forward? Or are they ad-hoc and not strategically focused? A careful review could uncover important opportunities to harness the team's energy around a common mission.

Risk Register

The risk register provides a comprehensive view of the organization's risks, including those related to both cybersecurity and the organization more broadly. Insights from a review of the risk register include:

1. **The business's perspective on current cybersecurity risks:** The risk register may include a specific section on cybersecurity risks, which can provide valuable insights into the organization's vulnerabilities and areas of concern. Spend some time validating whether these risks are still applicable and prioritize your efforts to ensure that your cybersecurity strategic plan is aligned with the organization's overall risk management strategy.

2. **Understanding the organization's risk tolerance:** The risk register may also provide information on what risks the organization has historically chosen to accept. This information may inform your own thinking about priorities and validate assumptions about areas you are considering focusing effort.

3. **Prioritizing cybersecurity initiatives:** The risk register may highlight specific cybersecurity risks that your organization considers a high priority. By understanding these priorities, you can ensure that your cybersecurity strategic plan addresses these risks and that your efforts are aligned with the organization's objectives.

4. **Identifying opportunities for collaboration:** The risk register might highlight important opportunities for collaboration with other departments or teams within the organization. By identifying areas where cybersecurity risks intersect with other types of risks, you can work with other teams to develop integrated risk management strategies that address these risks more effectively.

Information Technology and Cybersecurity Budget

These budgets can provide valuable insights into the organization's priorities and investment strategies and can help you align your cybersecurity strategic plan with the business's objectives. Insights from a review of these reports include:

1. **Understanding the historic areas of investment and spending norms:** You need to understand how the company is already spending money and what you have to work with. Equally important, though, is the importance of knowing what the company has historically avoided allocating resources toward. If there are missing tools, duplicate tools, or gaps in capabilities, as a leader, you'll want to know about that.

2. **Identifying investment priorities:** By reviewing the organization's prior budgets, you can identify its investment priorities and areas of focus. For example, you may discover large line items for infrastructure rehauls or important product updates. Knowing these priorities enables you to identify and advocate for certain investments from the perspective of your security team.

3. **Understanding resource constraints:** Prior budgets can also provide insights into the organization's resource constraints, including staffing levels or spending philosophies. For example, does your organization practice zero-based budgeting or require a business case for requests for resources?

4. **Clarity on cybersecurity budget ownership:** Does the cybersecurity team have a separate budget, or does it roll up to information technology? Understanding budget ownership may help you decipher the internal power dynamics and navigate future resource requests.

#2: Talk to the People Beyond Security

Cybersecurity is not just the responsibility of the cybersecurity team. It requires buy-in and support from other departments and stakeholders.

This means that cybersecurity leaders must avoid working in silos. As a leader, your job is to develop relationships and get feedback from other leaders to inform security objectives. For example, talking to IT and engineering may help you realize the organization has limited resources available to implement new cybersecurity technologies. Incorporating this constraint into your cybersecurity strategy, you are then able to prioritize which technologies to implement first.

By talking to other people across the business in your strategic planning process, you can:

- Gain a better understanding of the organization's goals and priorities,
- Stays informed about emerging technologies and threats,
- Identify key risks and challenges on a department-to-department level and develop a cybersecurity strategy that addresses them, and
- Gain buy-in and support from other departments for your cybersecurity strategy.

In our work at risk3sixty, we often hear security teams say, "I agree we should do more to understand the business's priorities, but how do we practically do that?" That is a fair question. So, to take this idea from theory to practical implementation, in the following sections I will provide some sample questions to ask the leaders across your business.

Executive Leadership Team (CEO, CFO, COO)

1. What is the overall business strategy of the organization, and how does it align with the industry trends?
2. How does the organization plan to differentiate itself from competitors, and what are the key success factors in achieving this differentiation?
3. What are the primary customer segments, and how does the organization plan to meet their needs?
4. What are the growth targets for the organization, and how does the organization plan to achieve them?
5. What are the potential risks and challenges to the organization's business strategy, and how are they being addressed?

Chief Information Officer/Chief Technology Officer

1. How does the organization's technology strategy and product roadmap align with the overall business strategy?
2. How has cybersecurity historically supported the technology organization? What should we do more of? What should we do less of?
3. What are the key technology trends that will impact the organization's industry, and how is the organization preparing for them?
4. How does the organization ensure that its technology investments align with business priorities?
5. How does the organization measure the effectiveness of its technology investments in supporting the business strategy?

Sales and Marketing

1. How does the organization's cybersecurity posture impact our ability to sell to potential customers?
2. How can we communicate our cybersecurity practices and certifications to potential customers to differentiate ourselves from competitors?

3. Are there any particular industries or customer segments where cybersecurity is a critical factor in the purchasing decision?
4. How can we leverage cybersecurity as a selling point for our products and services?
5. What role does marketing play in communicating cybersecurity-related updates and incidents to customers and stakeholders, and how can we improve our communication strategies?

Legal and Compliance

1. What are the organization's key legal and compliance obligations related to cybersecurity, and how are we currently meeting them?
2. Do we currently have contracts with customers that require our organization to meet cybersecurity or privacy obligations? How do we track new and existing requirements?
3. How does the legal and compliance team work with other departments, such as IT and cybersecurity, to ensure that legal and compliance obligations related to cybersecurity are being met?
4. What are the potential legal and financial risks associated with a cybersecurity incident, and how can we mitigate these risks? Have there been prior cybersecurity incidents or litigation related to cybersecurity?
5. How can the legal and compliance team be involved in developing cybersecurity policies and procedures to ensure that they align with legal and compliance obligations?

#3: Document and Validate Your Ideas with Peers

After you gather all of this information, you are going to need to get your thoughts on paper and validate your assumptions with peers. There will be a lot of ideas, incomplete data, misunderstandings, and missed side conversations that you will need to clear up before you can finalize your team's purpose. Sharing your proposed strategic objectives and seeking feedback from your peers will help refine your thinking.

Your peers will have insights and perspectives that you may not have considered and will have the secondary benefit of gaining buy-in from your peers across the organization. This can help build allies for your cybersecurity strategy when you need them later—which comes in handy if you need to request resources or work on cross-functional projects.

If you operate in a silo, you will have blind spots. When defining your team's purpose, you can avoid blind spots by stepping out of your silo. The purpose statement is the thing everything else will align to—both within your team and outside of it—so it is worth getting this part right.

Even Geniuses Get It Wrong if They Don't Collaborate

Even if you are a genius, you still need to collaborate.

John Lasseter, the creative genius behind the Toy Story franchise, can attest. He almost ruined the characters of Woody and Buzz Lightyear during development of the first *Toy Story* movie.

In the early 1990s, Pixar was a relatively small animation studio that had yet to produce a full-length feature film. The company had been working on *Toy Story* for several years, but the story and characters had not yet fully developed.

At one point in the development process, director John Lasseter gathered the entire team together, presented storyboards and character designs, and encouraged the team to give feedback and ideas.

The team hated Buzz Lightyear.

During the feedback session, Lasseter's team suggested that the character should be funny, not the serious, traditional action hero he was being presented as. To bring more life to the character, the team suggested that the script play up the idea that Buzz believed himself to be a real space ranger rather than just a toy.

This suggestion may have saved the movie, which went on to gross over $370 million worldwide and become one of the most beloved animated movies of all time.

Yes, sharing your ideas can be scary. It makes you feel vulnerable. But it will also build trust and strengthen your plans. Writing and distributing your ideas gives your team something they can challenge. When ideas are challenged, they grow stronger. This will make your purpose and vision stronger.

Do not skip this step.

Example Purpose Statements

If you are looking for inspiration, here are a couple of examples of purpose statements that do a great job mapping back to business objectives.

GitLab

GitLab serves thousands of companies globally and makes their security and compliance mission and vision available on the internet. Their mission statement offers a great example of a clear focus on risk management, customer trust, and revenue generation.[10]

---

[10] The following mission statement excerpt was from May 2022:
https://about.gitlab.com/handbook/security/#-security-vision-and-mission

Risk3sixty

Here is our security program mission statement at risk3sixty.

Business and Security Objectives

- **Lead By Example**
  Risk3sixty feels that it is important that we lead by example. Achieving certification is our signal to our industry that we take security, privacy, and continuity seriously and find real value in the services that we recommend to clients. We desire to poise the organization as thought leaders who "practice what we preach".

← Customer trust

- **Inspire Trust**
  We want to inspire trust with our clients. We will leverage formal certification of our security, privacy, and continuity program to boost company reputation and give customer's confidence.

risk management →

- **Keep Data Safe**
  Our clients and employees expect that we keep their data safe. We have chosen to implement a formalized security, privacy, and continuity program to reduce the risk of a potential security breach or disruptive continuity event.

- **The Speed of Security**
  It is essential that our firm can bring new products, features, and services to customers without sacrificing security. We operate on principles of security by design, we enable customers by making security features available to clients by default (e.g., SSO, MFA), and reduce roadblocks to decision making through clear communication and transparency.

← reduce complexity

No More Cynicism

There is a fate worse than death. Ask Sisyphus.

Everyday Sisyphus labors, rolling a giant boulder to the top of a large hill. And every night, the boulder tumbles back to where it began that morning.

No progress. No purpose. Day in and day out. For eternity.

This is the cruel fate of the doomed king Sisyphus described in ancient Greek legend. A fate worse than death. Eternal futility.

In preparing for this book, I interviewed over 250 security leaders and hundreds of security team members. And many of them felt they were dealt hands much like Sisyphus. They showed up every day, labored in vain, and had very little to show for it. Like Sisyphus rolling the boulder up the hill, they were engaged in futile efforts—and futility can lead to dangerous cynicism. The kind of cynicism that breeds resentment, undermines teams, and works against the Company's goals.

But it is in your power to avoid these leaders' fates.

You can give your security teams the gift of clarity. You can help them describe how their work in security directly ties to the success of the business. You can help their work mean something. And that can change everything.

Often, security teams feel out of the loop on how and why decisions about the security program are being made by the executive team. I often heard statements like "The leadership team doesn't really care about security," or "The business never gives our team the resources we need to secure the company." That kind of disconnect between the business and the security team is poisonous.

That is why a clear vision is the first step in revolutionizing the performance and culture of your security team.

When Stacy was able to paint a clear picture of her vision for her security engineering team, she did the hard work every leader must do. She was able to understand the business's perspective, tie it to the security team's work, and clearly articulate it to her team. As a result, her team went from cynical and misdirected to clear and motivated. They learned to love their work again.

If you can do that for your team. They will learn to love their work again too.

No more cynicism.

Download the Tools

Download the tools referenced in this chapter to document your team's Purpose at www.risk3sixty.com/stos

Download it
by scanning this
(you won't
regret it)

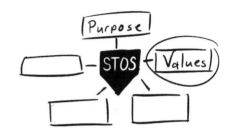

CHAPTER 3

VALUES

Executive Summary

Leaders establish principles and hold their teams accountable to acceptable rules of behavior. In this chapter, we will cover how leaders can establish principles and values that enforce a strong team culture. Once you feel confident in your defined values, we will cover examples and provide tools to help you integrate values in practical ways that reinforce the culture you are building.

Self-Assessment Questions

☐	What are the core values of your company?
☐	What are the core values of your security team?
☐	Are the security team's core values documented and shared with the team?
☐	Do you integrate your team's core values into processes like hiring, performance reviews, and decision-making?
☐	Could every team member recite your team's core values?

It was 6 a.m.

We had run over fifty miles. Fifty miles. I had been sitting in the same sweaty clothes for six hours. My feet hurt. My back hurt. There were twelve people crammed in our van as part of the two-hundred-mile relay race—and every one of them felt the same. Worse—we had eighteen hours and another 150 miles to go.

This was the low point.

It had been dark outside the entire race. Soul-sucking darkness. There was no scenery to enjoy outside—just blackness as our feet hit the road. No one was in a talkative mood. We all should have been sleeping, not packed in a van. And certainly not running a two-hundred-mile relay race.

I remember sitting in that van, shoulder to shoulder with my teammates, realizing I couldn't lie down. Realizing that I couldn't sleep. Just sit, then run, then do it again. For twelve more hours.

Is there any way we can get out of this? I thought to myself. I was miserable, I knew my team was miserable, and it was my fault. I was embarrassed. These were people I worked with. Were they mad at me? Did this make me look foolish? Probably. I was the one who had dragged my team here with me.

So, how did we get here? The same way we get here *every year*.

Our Annual "Grit" Event

Doing hard things is a cultural artifact specific to risk3sixty. I do not think that most teams can or should do the things we do. Your team will have its own unique culture and traditions. That's a good thing. But doing hard things like adventure races is part of our cultural story. So, somehow it works.

Grit is one of our core values.

Many of our employees come from a military background, including two West Point graduates on our leadership team. So naturally, we tend to see value in shared adversity. In 2017, we decided to do something in the physical world to represent our core values: run a hundred-mile relay race. This was in our very early startup days when we only had six people on the team.

When you have six people, you can afford to do crazy things. And at that stage, sometimes, ideas snowball into reality. We decided to run the race, and we invited some clients to join in so we could fill out the team. We ended up entering two teams of seven, ran the relay, and then came back and did it all again the next year.

That's how the tradition began.

By the third year, we decided to find a two-hundred-mile relay race. The hundred had been bad—and yet, somehow, not bad enough. Wanting to push ourselves a little harder this time, we put together a team of twelve and entered the race. Then we did the math. Each person could choose their own distance—in other words, they could literally run their own race—but on average, we'd each be running roughly a half-marathon when all was said and done.

It was an ambitious goal, but one we were confident we could handle. Through both our work and the previous hundred-mile relays, we'd learned that doing hard things together brought us together. Conquering adversity as a group promotes cohesion, a lesson the military understands well. The people who've participated in these relay races with us still talk about them. If I run into someone I haven't seen in a while, their experience running the relay with us always comes up. Given our emphasis on grit, the relays are a tangible symbol of how we live our values.

The Struggle is on Purpose

The relay race began at midnight, and we were all amped up to start, since the first few legs usually go off without a hitch. We took turns going all in, and then we got back in the van to rest and get warm.

That's when reality started to sink in. Once you're back in that van, you begin to realize how sweaty and disgusting you are—and that you won't get a chance to shower until the entire race is finished. Best you can do is change your clothes and try not to offend anyone with your body odor.

By about six in the morning, we were all flagging. What had started out as a funny and exciting challenge now felt like a terrible mistake. Sitting in the dark, we all stared at the clock, willing the next twelve hours to go by faster so we could pack up and go home.

But just as our misery was at its highest, the sun slowly peeked over the horizon, and the day began. As the sun rose, we sipped our coffees, had breakfast, and found new life. We know this moment was coming—as it does every year—and it engrained in our team the knowledge that hard things end and perseverance pays off. We could do this. We'd already managed it this far—and now it was time to finish what we started.

And that's exactly what we did. That is what we always do.

The struggle is on purpose. The point isn't for any of us to suffer, but by choosing this kind of controlled adversity that we could work through together, we knew what we would get as a result: a stronger team culture.

When the last runner on our team crossed that finish line about twelve hours later—two hundred sweaty and exhausting miles from the start—it reinforced our culture and gave us a tangible symbol of why grit matters. Even more, it gave us confidence—both in ourselves and our team members. No one groaned about what a bad idea this was. Instead, we were making plans to do it again next year (we eventually settled for a Spartan Race in 2023).

It feels good to live your values.

The pride and accomplishment in overcoming a challenge together easily outweigh any temporary suffering. When pain is in service of meaning and purpose, people learn get to the other side and have clarity that the hardship was valuable.

The sun always comes up again.

Fulfilling our roles as leaders means taking our teams on a journey. Great business leaders establish intentional values and work to breathe life into them. Your values have to come alive. They have to be more than a poster on the wall. It is up to you to figure out how to live them every day. How to make them real.

While not every company should run two hundred miles together, leaders should intentionally establish values, figure out ways to live up to them, and work to get their teams on board. The way you run your literal or metaphorical race has to be by design, not by accident. Every leader can be intentional about the symbols and activities they leverage to rally a team around the culture.

Culture is the invisible force that guides the behavior of every team. You don't get it with ping-pong tables, cool swag, and free snacks. It is built and reinforced by *values*. You know a team with strong values because they are teams with an abundance of accountability and mutual respect. Bought-in team members respect each other's time, meet commitments, strive for excellence, and are all on the same page about what needs to get done and why.

Teams with great culture do the little things right. They show up to meetings on time, they listen when another person is speaking, they take notes, they do their assignments on time and with quality, they ask hard questions, they trust each other enough to disagree, they respect personal and private boundaries, they are professionals, and they take initiative.

As a leader on your team, you have an amazing opportunity. You can create the best work environment that you or any of your team members have ever been a part of. It just takes desire and a little creativity. If you are reading this book—I know you have the desire. Now let's talk about how to get creative and make it happen.

Why Values Matter

Every team has values. In most cases, those values evolve organically and aren't written down, but they exist. For some teams, their values include negativity, cynicism, showing up late to meetings, and missing commitments. For other teams, their values may include excellence, teamwork, positive attitudes, accountability, and quality. Whether your values are formal or implicit, whether your values are harmful or healthy, those values drive your culture.

Core values are the fundamental beliefs and principles that guide the behavior and decision-making processes of your team. Sometimes they are unspoken, but they are always present. Values are your team's default settings, your team's muscle memory for behavior. They shape a company's culture, influencing both the actions of employees and the way the entire business operates.

For these reasons, a formal, documented, and discussed set of values can go a long way toward building a unified team culture and position your security organization for greater success within the company.

Clearly defined core values provide a sense of purpose and direction for everyone in the organization. Written values act as a compass that guides decision-making, define the company's brand, and set the tone for the workplace environment. Further, written values give leaders something to point back to when someone doesn't live up to the team's expectations. In all these ways, values add clarity to behaviors that might otherwise be unspoken or hard to measure.

For example, as remote or hybrid work environments have become more prominent, many companies have struggled to maintain a cohesive culture. Often, these challenges are correlated with fuzzy or poorly defined values. Just like with purpose, values help to get everyone rowing in the same direction. A culture with fuzzy values isn't well-equipped to respond to a remote worker who works in a silo and doesn't communicate. However, a culture where teamwork, collaboration, and communication are clearly defined values can point to these expectations when that person is reluctant to come out of their silo and support their fellow teammates. Values set expectations and drive the rules of acceptable behavior.

Core values also play a critical role in attracting and retaining talent. Once you have defined your values, you have something to measure potential team members against. As a result, it's easier to keep the bad fits out and bring the good fits in. A team of high performers all aligned with your stated values creates a sense of shared purpose, fosters a stronger sense of community, and leads to a much higher retention rate.

This is how you create a team that loves where they work.

As a security leader, you have the unique opportunity to give your team something to believe in, principles to stand for, and a system of internal team accountability.

This is your most powerful leadership tool.

But be careful: Values aren't just words on the wall. It takes work for your values to work for you. You must integrate your values into key business processes, hold people accountable to them, and remind people they are important.

In the following sections, we'll explore four key ways to establish and drive values in a practical and meaningful way.

Value Driver #1: Hiring

Hiring great people is the number one thing you can do to improve the performance of your team. As a security leader, you must bring in great people—people who are not only talented, but who bring the right values and energy to your team. And you have to stop the bad apples at the door.

As Steve Jobs famously said, "A players hire A players, and B players hire C players."[11] You want to hire cultural A players who attract other A players. Do not compromise on the type of individuals you allow to be a part of your team.

Hiring great people starts with the belief that you deserve to be surrounded by great people and that it is possible to find them—because both are true, whether you believe it or not. The world is full of high-quality individuals with great attitudes who are an ideal cultural fit seeking jobs for companies just like yours right now. Fight to find them, and you will transform the culture of your organization forever.

At risk3sixty, our internal code word for these people is "Strange Renegades," a term we borrowed from thought leader Verne Harnish as a way of saying we are serious about our cultural identity and holding each other accountable to our core values. According to Harnish,

> [When it comes to hiring people] it's crucial that you start playing chess sooner rather than later. Think of "the A-Team" of action television fame—a ragtag group of *renegades* bringing their individual and unique talents, personalities, and strengths together to act on the side of good . . . [You want to] hire people who are downright *strange* . . . if your competitive advantage depends on your people creating something valuable and distinctive, then your workforce can't be normal.[12]

You deserve to work with your own team of Strange Renegades, people who bring positive energy to work, who are self-managing, who lift the team up and never tear the team down. If you define your values, you can build this kind of team. We have been able to hire great team members through a strong recruiting and hiring process.

---

[11] Walter Isaacson. *Steve Jobs*. (New York: Simon & Schuster): 2011.
[12] Verne Harnish. *Scaling Up: How a Few Companies Make It . . . and Why the Rest Don't*. (Miami: Gazelles Inc.). 2014. p. 65–66. Emphasis added.

Of course, building a team is not a passive process. Recruiting must be a core competency, which means being proactive about attracting and enticing the very best people to interview at your company.

Here are a few of the things that have worked for our team.

Establish a Brand

Establish a strong employer brand within the security community to attract top talent. That includes a strong personal brand and a strong company brand. I've found success on this front through social media, a quarterly digital magazine, blogging, lectures, events, videos, and training. Be sure to showcase your company culture, values, and opportunities for professional growth and development. If you want to attract top talent, you must do things that other security teams are unable or unwilling to do to get noticed.

Contribute to the Security Community

Encourage your team to actively participate and engage with professional networks, industry events, and online forums related to cybersecurity. This can include sharing insights, expertise, and thought leadership through blog posts, whitepapers, or speaking engagements. Some of my favorite local events include local BSides chapters, local chapters of professional organizations like ISACA or ISSA, and the occasional risk3sixty-hosted meetup. By actively contributing to the community, your organization can gain visibility, build relationships, and attract candidates who are passionate about cybersecurity and value community involvement.

On Campus

Here is another valuable strategy for attracting young talent: get involved with local colleges and universities through on-campus recruiting activities. Consider doing more than just job fairs by attending student events, offering internships and co-op programs, guest lecturing, and building relationships with professors. At risk3sixty, we have formed partnerships with the Georgia Institute of Technology, the University of Georgia, and others that have made a huge difference in our ability to access talented students. By establishing a presence on campuses, you can connect with students who are pursuing relevant degrees or certifications and showcase the opportunities your organization offers in the cybersecurity field.

Nontraditional Educational Programs and Bootcamps

In addition to traditional educational institutions, nontraditional educational programs and boot camps are great places to recruit experienced candidates transitioning into cybersecurity. Partnering with these programs or sponsoring boot camp initiatives can help your organization tap into a diverse pool of talent from nontraditional backgrounds. I love people with nontraditional backgrounds because they bring a different perspective to the team, they have grit, and they are excited about breaking into the industry. We have found some of our best people in these sorts of programs.

Creative Guerilla Marketing

Guerilla marketing involves unconventional and creative strategies to promote your organization and attract potential candidates. This is a great opportunity to focus on low-cost tactics that create a memorable and unique brand experience. For example, try running a creative ad on LinkedIn, paying a professional videographer to make a team hype video, or hosting a hackathon. Anything that creates a memorable experience for potential candidates will give you a leg up in attracting awesome people to your team. At risk3sixty, we have created hype videos paired with team endurance races and gone all-in on creating free YouTube content for security practitioners. As a bonus, these activities create a fun opportunity for your current team to participate in creative activities outside of their day job.

Ultimately, it's your job to figure out a way to mobilize your team to attract talented individuals. That may mean that you have to work with corporate recruiting to help provide resources. Or it may mean that you need to give your security team the time and resources necessary to self-source team members. In either case, recruiting talented individuals should be a top priority for your security team.

Hiring Based on "GWC Core Values"

Once you start attracting the right people, you need to have a way to assess who will be a good fit. At risk3sixty, we get hundreds of job applications for every job we post. That means we have to be great at interviewing. My favorite way to make sure you hire the right people is the "GWC Core Values" methodology made popular by the book *Traction* by Gino Wickman and the business coaching organization EOS Worldwide.

The GWC Core Values hiring methodology helps companies find and hire candidates who are a good fit for their organization's culture by assessing whether they have the necessary "GWC" characteristics:

- **Get It:** Does the candidate have a clear understanding of the role they are applying for and the company's mission, vision, and values? In other words, do they "get" what the company is all about?

- **Want It:** Does the candidate have the passion and commitment to do the job well and thrive within the company culture?

- **Capacity to Do It:** Do they have the skills, knowledge, and experience necessary to perform the job duties effectively and successfully?

- **Core Values:** The candidate fits with your defined core values.

To implement the GWC Core Values hiring methodology, a company would first define its core values and the GWC criteria for the role they are hiring for. They would then use a combination of tools such as behavioral interviewing techniques, skills assessments, and reference checks to evaluate candidates based on the GWC criteria.

During the hiring process, the GWC Core Values methodology can help a company identify candidates who not only have the necessary skills and experience, but who also align with the company's culture and values. We have used the GWC Core Values as a basis for our hiring at risk3sixty since 2016.

Value Driver #2: Firing

Core values establish the nonnegotiables for behavior on your team. Values are the tangible attributes you hold your team accountable to. And when someone steps outside those established norms, it may be grounds for getting that person off the bus.

In *The Energy Bus*, thought leader Jon Gordon warns of the dangers of hiring people who aren't aligned to your team's values:

> If you want to be successful you have to be very careful about who is on your [team]. After all there are people who increase your energy and there are people who drain your energy. I call people who drain your energy vampires; they will suck the life out of you and your goals and vision if you let them.[13]

I agree—and I've seen it happen. If you want a highly successful team, build a team that aligns with your values. When everyone is aligned to a common mission with a common set of values, they will bring energy to each other and accomplish great things together.

This is the kind of culture you deserve. Teams where the people you work with energize you and make you happy. People that make you feel good, people that you are excited to see every day, people who bring a positive energy to the team.

Imagine coming to work full of energy, excited about the conversations you get to have with interesting and talented people. Imagine a whole team that exceeds your expectations, predicts each other's needs, and makes everyone on the team feel like they are on top of the world every day. You should strive to build a team like this. You *can* build a team like this.

One of the first steps to achieving this is to make sure everyone who is on your team *belongs* on your team. If you have someone on the team who you or your team dreads working with every day, get rid of them immediately. I don't care how talented they are. They are not worth it. If you allow these types of people to persist in your organization, they will attract more people like themselves and scare away the people you want to keep.

---

[13] Jon Gordon. *The Energy Bus: 10 Rules to Fuel Your Life, Work, and Team with Positive Energy. (New York: Wiley): 2007.*

I've learned this lesson from hard-earned experience. The hardest decisions I have ever had to make as a business leader have all had something to do with firing people. A million things go through your head when you need to let someone go. You think about their family, you think about your personal relationship with them, and you question yourself. But the truth is, if you are already considering firing someone, it is probably long overdue.

A few years ago, I had to make one of the most difficult decisions of my professional career when I fired an early team member and personal friend from risk3sixty. I wrestled with the decision for months because I knew that it would disrupt my company and would end our friendship. But I also knew that it was the right thing for our team, our clients, and the employee.

After some reflection, I realized that the employee did not fit the future of the company and was not living up to our core values. I also realized that the employee was also limiting himself by staying. He had bigger and better opportunities outside of risk3sixty, and we were both delaying the inevitable.

After the employee left the company, it became immediately obvious it was the right decision for both of us. Our culture improved, we experienced significant growth and maturity in several key areas, and the employee went off to take a leadership position at a different company.

Was it easy? Hell no. But looking back on the decision with the benefit of hindsight, it is clear that it was one of the most important decisions I have ever made as a leader. And it was a decision that only a leader can make. I owed it to my team to make the hard decision and to have the hard conversations to preserve our culture.

There will come a time, probably many times, where you will have to make hard decisions too. My suggestion is to act quickly and never let the wrong person stay on your bus.

Value Driver #3: Performance Reviews

Another way to keep values top of mind is to integrate your values into performance reviews. Including core values as a metric in your performance reviews demonstrates to your team that you take them seriously and plan to hold the team accountable. It also creates a valuable opportunity to formally discuss how each team member is (or is not) living up to the team's acceptable rules of behavior.

Jackie is the Head of Information Security at a large government contractor in Texas. She is a culture-first leader passionate about her team's values. As part of her role, Jackie has integrated a values assessment into her performance reviews and coaching conversations:

> Before every performance review, I ask our team members to rate themselves against each value. This is a self-assessment to consider how each person believes they are living up to our values. I also ask each manager to rate the person against our values and site-specific examples. Then, during the coaching session, the manager and the team member compares the result. This creates an opportunity for a great coaching session on how each person arrived at the score. And what I have found is that people are a lot harder on themselves than their managers.

By integrating values into formal coaching conversations, Jackie has created time and space for managers to have candid conversations about elements of performance that are often intangible.

One manager on Jackie's team described the experience in the following way:

> [A]t first it was awkward to have a conversation about our team's values. The meeting was a little clunky, and I didn't know how to approach it. But after a few minutes, I realized that talking about our values created an opportunity to have a deeper and more meaningful conversation than I have ever had as a manager. It also meant that our team members had to take the time to learn and understand our core values because they knew they would be measured against them. Now the whole team is in the habit of considering our values every day and in every big decision.

In this way, the core values became a central part of the performance review process, helping to ensure that team members were not only meeting their technical goals but also contributing to a culture of integrity, collaboration, and continuous improvement within the cybersecurity team.

Value Driver #4: Decision-Making

Leaders make a lot of decisions. Many of those decisions are difficult. But it is a lot easier to make difficult decisions if you have a framework built on sound principles.

Richard is the CEO of a managed services provider that helps organizations respond to and recover from security breaches. During a conversation together, he told me a story about a time he had to part ways with a client.

> We had a very large client that we had evidence was actively involved in a data breach. We notified the client and did not get a response. After our team could not get in touch with their team, I decided to call their CEO directly. After speaking with the CEO, he confirmed that they had a security breach. I told him that he would likely have to notify impacted customers, but he refused. I reminded him that his contracts and several regulations required him to notify customers. He made a lot of excuses and downplayed the event, but I knew it was the wrong thing to do.

Richard sat with the decision for a few days. He felt strongly that he would need to part ways with the client, but the client represented about 5 percent of Richard's revenue—a very large client. Still, Richard knew that if he did not act, it would set a poor example for his team, would be in conflict with his values, and could even lead to legal problems.

> I lost sleep for several nights. I tried to justify keeping them as a customer. I told myself that the revenue from the client paid for several employees on my team. I told myself that perhaps I did not have all the information and they were right not to disclose the breach. But in my heart, I knew it wasn't right. I grabbed a notebook and decided to compare my options against my core values. The analysis made it clear I had to part ways with this client.

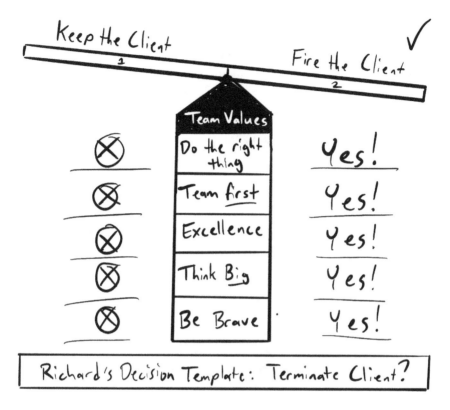

Keep the Client — 1
Fire the Client ✓ — 2

Team Values

⊗	Do the right thing	Yes!
⊗	Team first	Yes!
⊗	Excellence	Yes!
⊗	Think Big	Yes!
⊗	Be Brave	Yes!

Richard's Decision Template: Terminate Client?

Richard chose to terminate his relationship with the client. He introduced the client to a great attorney and an alternate service provider and parted on good terms.

> I knew that parting ways was the right thing to do. And after the relationship ended, I had several employees thank me for the decision. As it turns out, no one on our team was enthusiastic about the account. They were difficult to serve and often caused our team a lot of anxiety. Terminating with the client increased team morale and built a lot of trust. It wasn't easy at the time, but it was absolutely the right decision. The decision-making framework also gave me a way to explain the decision to our team and board of directors. It helped give me the confidence to move forward.

Leaders have to deliver bad news, hire and terminate employees, end client relationships, manage customer complaints, mediate conflict, make investment decisions on behalf of the company, and often navigate situations that feel like there is no good alternative.

These decisions are hard.

Values-based decision-making helps leaders clarify these moments and explain their decisions to others. If your question passes the values-based decision model, it is probably a good decision. People respect principled decision-making—even when they disagree with the decision itself.

Of course, you don't want to be the bottleneck for every decision either. As a leader, it's far better to empower your team to make decisions and operate autonomously. Values-based decision-making frameworks can empower your team by helping them make tough decisions without the need to escalate.

At risk3sixty, we have grown rapidly over the years. And through that growth, our team realized that we had to work consciously to maintain company culture. We wanted to ensure that everyone in the company was aligned with the organization's core values and had the skills to make decisions that were consistent with those values.

To achieve that goal, we implemented a management training program called the "Journeyman Program." The program was designed to train employees on leadership and decision-making skills and align their decision-making processes with the organization's core values.

The Journeyman Program consists of a series of modules that cover topics such as problem-solving, critical thinking, and decision-making. Each module includes a discussion of the organization's core values and how they relate to the decision-making process. The program also includes case studies and exercises to help employees practice their decision-making skills.

Managers who complete the Journeyman Program report feeling more confident in their ability to make decisions and more aligned with the organization's core values. Since implementing the program, we have noticed a significant improvement in the quality of decision-making across the organization, with middle managers feeling more empowered to take initiative. The program has also helped to foster a sense of community within the organization, bringing employees from different departments and levels of the organization together to participate in the same program.

Training your team on your organization's core values can help those team members make decisions that align with how you as the leader would make that decision, thus scaling the team's decision-making capabilities in several ways:

1. **Provides a shared understanding:** Everyone understands the organization's core values and how they relate to its mission and purpose. This shared understanding can serve as a foundation for making decisions that align with the leader's values and vision.

2. **Sets expectations:** Team members have a clear understanding of how decisions should be made. This can help them predict how the leader would decide and thus make decisions that are consistent with the organization's values and principles.

3. **Increases confidence:** When team members understand the values and how they relate to their work, they are more likely to feel confident in making decisions that align with those values.

4. **Enables delegation:** Team members are better equipped to make decisions on their own, without constant oversight from leadership. This enables leaders to delegate decision-making responsibilities and focus on other areas of the business.

A lot of leaders feel the pain of "decision fatigue" or get frustrated when their leaders are unable to take the initiative and act without their guidance. If you are feeling that kind of pain, this may be a good opportunity to train your emerging leaders to approach decision-making in the same way that you would. They can do it! And it will free you up to think more strategically and take the organization to the next level.

Exercise: A 5-Step Process to Define Your Core Values

If your team doesn't have a set of core values, it is up to you as the leader to kick off the process of getting values on paper.

This can feel difficult at first. After all, defining your culture and values requires a lot of thinking and creativity. The idea of culture itself is almost ethereal. It is hard to nail down. You know it when you see culture in action, but it is difficult to put into words. Especially simple words.

Culture also isn't something you can force on your team. You can't just disappear into the wilderness, come up with flashy core values, and expect your team to adopt them. It just doesn't work like that. You already have a culture, your team is already a part of it, and therefore they need to be a part of defining it—which can present its own set of challenges.

Bringing your team into the conversation involves considerable collaboration and consensus-building among team members. If defining culture is hard to articulate on your own, it's even harder to get everyone else on the team to agree to something so inherently ethereal. Each individual will have different perspectives, priorities, and beliefs, which can make it difficult to reach a shared understanding and agreement on the core values.

But while finding common ground and aligning everyone's viewpoints can be a complex, iterative process, there is good news: You do not have to do it alone. Here is a five-step process to help your team develop and define your core values:

1. **Individual brainstorming:** During this step, each team member engages in individual brainstorming to generate a list of potential core values. Encourage team members to think about their personal values, the elements most important to their team's success, and the desired culture they want to create. This phase allows for diverse perspectives and ideas to emerge.

2. **Values ranking:** After individual brainstorming, it's time to rank the generated values. Each team member can assign a score or rank to each value based on their personal preference and perceived importance. Use a rating scale or similar method that suits your team's dynamics. This step helps identify the values that resonate most with the team collectively.

3. **Shortlisting:** Based on the values ranking, shortlist the top values that received the highest scores or rankings. Focus on the values that are widely supported by the team and align with the team's goals and purpose. Consider the values that represent the desired behaviors, attitudes, and principles for the team to uphold.

4. **Ratifying:** Once you have shortlisted your values, it is time to ratify the selected core values. This involves bringing the team together to discuss and finalize the shortlisted values. Encourage open and transparent communication, allowing team members to express their perspectives and concerns. Seek consensus among team members and ensure

everyone has a voice in the decision-making process. Once the core values are agreed upon, document them formally as the team's core values.

5. **Implement and integrate:** The final step is to integrate your core values into your hiring, firing, performance review, decision-making, and any other meaningful processes your team finds relevant.

Don't settle until you've arrived at a set of core values that truly reflect the team's identity and aspirations. In other words, avoid being generic or superficial. Your core values need to be clear, specific, and meaningful. They should provide guidance and serve as a compass for decision-making and behavior. It can be challenging to articulate values in a way that is both concise and comprehensive, capturing the essence of what the team stands for—but as hard as it might seem in the moment, the effort is always worth it.

Finally, while your core values should be enduring and stand the test of time, teams and organizations also evolve. As a result, your values may need to adapt to new challenges, opportunities, and cultural shifts as well. How do you strike the balance between stability and flexibility when defining something as fundamental as values?

Leaders Set the Tone

Udonis Haslem spent twenty seasons wearing a Miami Heat jersey—his entire NBA career on one team, in the city where grew up. He was team captain for sixteen seasons and helped win three NBA championships. Now, his jersey will forever hang from the rafters in the Heat's home arena, next to Miami Heat legends like Alonzo Mourning, Tim Hardaway, Shaquille O'Neal, Chris Bosh, and Dwyane Wade.

A retired jersey is an honor bestowed upon few athletes, one typically reserved for the most elite performers in their sport. But what stands out about Haslem is this: his stats don't stand out. In fact, they are barely mediocre.

Udonis went undrafted out of college and spent the 2002 season in France. In 2003, he joined the Miami Heat, where he averaged 7.5 points and 6.6 rebounds per game during his twenty-year NBA career. During the final nine years of that career, Haslem barely earned any time on the court. He played about ten minutes per game in the 2014–15 season and averaged less than one minute per game in his last few seasons. He never made an All-Star team. He never even made player of the week.

So, if numbers don't define his Heat legacy, then what does?

Udonis's leadership.

"He was the glue. A lot of people get lost in the stats, who averages the most, but he was the glue for everybody. . . . And I feel like the glue guys are the most important guys on a team," said Heat Center Bam Adebayo.[14] For twenty years, Udonis was famous for his intensity, his colorful language, and most importantly—the way he set the tone in the locker room and off the court.

For example, Udonis had a tradition of holding secret one-on-one games with Heat stars Dwyane Wade and Jimmy Butler, where he played with renowned intensity. While most NBA stars might play at 50 to 75 percent in practice, Udonis would give it full effort. Why? Not for ego. But to make his team better. To keep the team's star players sharper. To keep the team's intensity high. And the culture tangible. As Haslem said in a profile on him on NBA.com,

> "I want these guys to understand that I care about them as human beings, not just basketball players or people that can win games for me or people that can bring a lot of notoriety to the organization," Haslem says. "Before I even get into anything that has to do with basketball, I approach you as a human being and as a person and build that equity with you. And then we can get into the basketball sh**."[15]

Udonis wasn't on the coaching staff, but he was more than a player. Udonis was a culture guy. A glue guy. A lead by example guy. A hold you accountable guy. A make you better guy. And a culture guy.

That's the kind of leadership that gets your jersey retired.

---

[14] Tim Reynolds. "Heat Retire Udonis Haslem's No. 40 Jersey." *NBA.com*. January 19, 2024. https://www.nba.com/news/heat-retire-udonis-haslem-40-jersey
[15] Couper Moorhead. "The Man in the Locker Room: Scenes from the 20-Year Career of Udonis Haslem, the Undrafted Player Who Became the Heart of a Franchise." *NBA.com*. Accessed February 19, 2024. https://www.nba.com/heat/news/scenes-20-year-career-udonis-haslem

You Have a Choice

I get that talking about core values might seem unnatural. Maybe you feel like it's not your place to talk about values. Maybe you don't know how to start the conversation. Maybe you are afraid of how your team will react when you want to talk about the "mushy stuff."

But look, here's the truth: It is your job as a leader to set the tone of your team. Period.

So, security leaders, you have a choice here. You can do nothing. You can let the culture on your team evolve on its own. You can let the person with the strongest personality dictate the culture. You can let cynicism rein. And you can let your culture hinder progress.

Going down that path is not pretty. It is uninspiring. Lukewarm at best.

Or you can take ownership of the culture on your team. You can build a team full of excellent people who are excited to come to work every day. A team that is full of good energy, fighting for each other, and fighting for the business.

Going down that path is bright. That's the place I want to work. And the good news is that you can build that kind of place.

All you have to do is set the tone for the team.

Download the Tools

Download the tools referenced in this chapter to document your team's Values at www.risk3sixty.com/stos

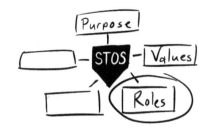

CHAPTER 4

ROLES

Executive Summary

Leaders ensure the right people are doing the right job to accomplish the mission. In this chapter, we will cover (1) how to clarify your role and spend your time, (2) how to design security governance that ensures influence and drives decision making, and (3) how to design a security team operating model that ensures the right people are in the right seat doing the right jobs.

Self-Assessment Questions

☐	Do you have a seat at the table with peer executives at your company?
☐	Is your opinion valued, or do you feel marginalized?
☐	Do you have a venue to bring up issues, ask for budget, and get things approved?
☐	Can every person on your team answer the following questions: o What elements of the security program am I responsible for? o What are the key performance indicators for each area I am responsible for? o Who do I report to? Who reports to me?

> ☐ Do you think that all the roles required to run a great security program are assigned to someone on your team? Are there gaps in your program? How do you know?

Security leaders don't have the clout.

We don't have the relationships. We haven't done the work to build trust and credibility. We aren't viewed as peers among our fellow C-Suite-level executives. We aren't attached to the business's strategy. We can't get the budget. We can't get the resources. And as a result, a lot of us walk around feeling cynical and frustrated. It hurts, but that's the truth.

If you don't believe me, take a poll at the next security conference you attend.

And look, I'm not saying those feelings of frustration don't have merit. Because they do. Many businesses don't take security seriously enough, even with all the headlines in the news. It is disappointing when executives keep their heads in the sand and pretend it will never happen to them.

But we can't do much about how other people think, can we? It's not useful.

Instead, let's focus on what we can do as security leaders. The things we can do to make the biggest impact on our team and our company. The things we can do to position ourselves as people of influence inside the organization. The things we can do to win hearts and minds.

That is what this chapter is all about. Why? Because organizational design is power.

Organizational Design Is Power

Matt is in charge of a team of fifty-two people.

He inherited the team when he accepted the CISO role at a $4 billion digital product company. He also inherited the organizational structure. The culture.

The reputation. The cybersecurity roadmap. And the political clout of his predecessor.

"I was excited. This team was about twice the size of my last team. But it was also the first time I had ever inherited the work of someone else. I didn't hire this team. I didn't build the culture. It was a new challenge," Matt told me.

After about three months, Matt started to realize there were major problems. His budget still wasn't approved, two big projects had stalled, and it was not clear what his team members were working on every day.

"At my last company, I had regular one-on-ones with the executive team. I had built my team one-by-one over about seven years. We had a great culture, a great team, and a lot of respect throughout the company. It just wasn't like that here," Matt said. "So, I knew I had to go to work making some big changes. I had to change how I planned to spend my time, my relationship with the leadership team, and my team's structure. If I wanted to make progress, it was less about cybersecurity maturity and more about how I planned to reposition the cybersecurity function inside the company."

Over the next three years, Matt transformed the design of the cybersecurity function. He worked hard to build relationships with the executive team and to understand the company's objectives. He also restructured the cybersecurity team to fill the most important roles and drive accountability.

"I honestly considered quitting. But I didn't think that was the right thing to do. Quitting was the easy path, not the right path. Organizational change is hard and time-consuming. Over the last three years, we have updated the governance structure, reorganized our team, and worked hard to make sure everyone understands their roles," Matt said. "Today, I have a great relationship with the executive leadership team, we have built an amazing security leadership program, and we are making great progress on our cybersecurity roadmap. I have the time to get out of the weeds and think strategically. We are working on the fun stuff now."

Does Matt's journey sound familiar? It does for a lot of us. And that's why the "Roles" part of the Security Team Operating System (STOS) is so important. After reading this chapter, you will have the playbook to accomplish three things:

1. How to clarify your role and spend your time

2. How to design security governance that ensures influence and drives decision making, and

3. How to design a security team operating model that ensures the right people are in the right seat doing the right jobs.

Let's get started.

4 Core Competencies of a Security Leader

Have you ever seen the movie *Rocky II*? It's the one where Rocky fights Apollo Creed in a rematch, after Creed narrowly beat Rocky in the first movie. One of my favorite scenes in the movie is when Rocky is torn between his obligations as a husband and his passion for boxing.

The scene goes like this:

Adrian (Rocky's wife) lies in the hospital bed, near death after complications from childbirth. Rocky, filled with worry and desperation, sits by her side, his emotions raw. Missing days of training to be by his wife's side. Adrian eventually regains consciousness, her voice feeble yet resolute as she implores Rocky, "Win." Her words, though faint, carry the weight of the pair's shared dreams and struggles, igniting a renewed fire within Rocky's spirit. And thus begins the famous training montage in *Rocky II*.

Rocky has clarity. He knows exactly who he is. He knows what he has to do. And he does it.

Do you know that feeling?

The feeling from going to unsure to sure. From confused to absolutely certain. Man, that's a powerful feeling. That's the power of clarity.

About six years into my career as a CEO and entrepreneur, I was introduced to a coaching program run by Dan Sullivan called "Strategic Coach." Sullivan is a legend in the business community, where he is often referred to as "the Coach's Coach." Alumni and members of his program include Gino Wickman (author of *Traction* and inventor of the Entrepreneur Operating System), Dr. Benjamin Hardy (best-selling author and speaker), Joe Polish (author and founder of Genius Network), and hundreds of other successful entrepreneurs.

One of the tools in Dan's program is called "Unique Ability." The goal of the tool is to help leaders better understand themselves as people and business leaders. The exercises within this tool are not easy to complete. They require a lot of deep thinking and introspection. But through that tool, and through many other similar tools I've used since then, I have come to understand that a leader must first understand themselves and their role before they can do a good job leading others.[16]

If you don't, bad things happen.

Leaders who are confused about how they should focus their time lose confidence and become indecisive. They don't know what to tell their teams. Their messages are mixed. And as a result, their team loses confidence too. If a team loses confidence, great people start to leave. The culture falls apart. The team crumbles.

Leaders who are clear and confident, like Rocky, have clarity in purpose. They train hard, they focus their effort, and they win.

That's why *team-level* confidence and clarity starts with *you-level* confidence and clarity.

This means asking some difficult questions:

- What are the things that only I can do?
- What things give me energy? What things drain my energy?
- Based on the list above, which tasks should I delegate?
- Do I have the right team members in the right roles to enable delegation?
- How will leveling up my capabilities create opportunities for my team?

Don't put off these questions. Why? Because your team can only rise as high as their leader, and it could be you holding your team back. You own fears and doubts could be preventing progress. So, you must level up your game to bring the security team up. *It starts with you.*

This begs the question: What should your role look like?

---

[16] You can try this tool out for yourself at https://uniqueability.com/. I highly recommend it.

In my experience, there are four core competencies that a security leader should focus their time on. These four areas provide a framework for your role as a security leader—and grant you permission to delegate everything else. Remember, by delegating, you are giving people on your team the opportunity to take on new and exciting roles.

Competency #1: Building a Strong Relationship with the Executive Team

The best security leaders I have ever worked with have the respect of their peers on the executive team. And like any healthy relationship, respect and trust is earned through a mutual commitment to solving hard problems and showing up consistently over time—probably for years.

For example, Leigh is one of the most respected security leaders I have ever worked with. He has an amazing instinct for business. When I first started working with him, he explained to me in detail his company's business model, revenue streams, and competitors, and then he accurately predicted his company's growth prospects over the next five years. He schooled me on the business's current stage of growth and where security fit in at that stage. He also knew the top priorities for other departments like finance and sales. He was a master, and everyone acknowledged it.

"I talk to people in other departments every day," Leigh told me. "I like to understand what is going on in their world and what is going on across the business. I don't want anything from them, I just want their perspective."

What did his credibility earn him?

Once I was at Leigh's office and the CEO dropped by. This took me by surprise, but I would come to learn that this was a common occurrence. They would discuss topics ranging from leadership and product roadmap to their weekend plans. These conversations turned into a strong working relationship. As a result, when Leigh needed to make an ask on behalf of the security team—he usually got what he needed. Leigh understood the value of building strong relationships with the executive team.

Do you have these kinds of relationships across your business?

Competency #2: Hiring and Building a Management Team

Every leader must surround themselves with quality individuals. And ultimately, no one can own this responsibility except for you.

- You own the hiring of great people based on your team values (Chapter 3).
- You own making sure those great people are in the right seat, doing the right job (this chapter, read on!).
- You own helping those people set and execute on important goals (Chapter 6).

One of my good friends, David, has made a career by building and scaling security teams. "I look for roles where I am the first security leadership hire. I love that part of the journey because you get to define the future of the function," David said.

In David's last role, he joined a private equity–backed company that was consolidating six companies into a single corporation.

"The goal was to take six distinct companies that were historically running separate security programs and combine them into one entity. We wanted to take security from a decentralized product-based function to a centralized shared service. But I literally had no team. I had to build it from scratch. That's why I took the job!" David told me.

David used elements of the Security Team Operating System to define values, design a security team operating model, and scale his team.

"For the first few months, almost all of my time was spent designing my organization structure, creating a hiring plan, and hiring competent managers I could trust. I knew hiring a great management team was an important step, otherwise, I would get pulled into the weeds," David said.

Competency #3: Creating Purpose and Alignment

Once you have the right crew on the boat, the next step is to get everyone rowing in the same direction. That's where purpose and alignment come in (see

Chapter 2). As the leader, you must beat the drum and keep communicating the team's purpose.

Sarah is the director of security at a large bank. Her planning process starts in June each year and requires that she coordinate across three teams. "Every year, we create a cybersecurity strategic plan that nests neatly within the company's strategic plan for the next year," Sarah said.

By October, she has a final draft of the plan for the following year. At this point, she begins to socialize this plan with her management team so they can begin the goal setting process for the following year.

> It takes a lot of effort to get the whole team in perfect alignment. It starts with me understanding how our plan fits in with the company's plans, then I have to get my management team on board, then they work with their team to set individual goals under that. But in the end, it keeps us all on the exact same page and working toward the exact same objectives. Then, we have quarterly performance updates to check in on progress and pivot if there have been any big changes.

As you can see from Sarah's example, purpose and clarity must come from the top. That is why it is a job only you can do. *That is the core of the Security Team Operating System.*

Competency #4: Defining and Growing Team Culture

As your team grows, you will lose your span of control. When that happens, you must rely on culture.

Randall has a security team of two hundred people. "There are people on my team that I only see a few times a year. I didn't interview them. And as much as I would like to, I don't know them that well. Our team is just too big!" Randall told me. "The only way to ensure a team as big as ours is all on the same page is by creating a culture that establishes clear boundaries on what is right and what is wrong."

To do that, Randall and his team established a set of core values that his whole team has embraced. "We are far from perfect. I mean, people make mistakes all the time. But when someone makes a mistake, they self-correct because they know it is not in alignment with how our team operates. That's the benefit of strong values. It kind of creates a self-healing machine," Randall said.

I sat in on Randall's weekly all-hands meeting. Randall showed up early, welcomed team members as they joined the meeting, and seemed to know personal details about a surprising number of the people gathered in the room. They also started the meeting with team member highlights from the prior week. The meeting was just one way Randall's team embedded values into their everyday behaviors.

"I'm the culture guy," Randall said. "It permeates all aspects of my job. The energy I bring to meetings, how I treat people in casual interactions, and what behaviors I accept in the office—all of it matters. Your team will take their cues from you and adjust their behavior to match yours."

Culture is tone from the top.

This Is Your Permission to Lead

I know you are working hard. Very hard. Maybe too hard.

Maybe you are stuck in the weeds, doing a thousand tasks that feel urgent and important. Answering an email, getting ready for a board presentation, another audit, another vendor meeting, managing conflicts. Then you look up and it has been six weeks, a year, three years. Sometimes we just need the reminder to step back and remember what is most important.

And I hope that this is that reminder.

Give yourself the permission to challenge your thinking about how you should be spending your team as a leader. Your team needs you to think about these things. Because if you don't, who will?

Governing Functions of a Security Team

Do you remember what I said at the beginning of this chapter?

"Security leaders don't have the clout," I said. And I stand by that. You probably don't have the clout. You probably don't have the relationships. But we are about to change that.

So many of the problems inside the cybersecurity function can be resolved if you are strategic about how you position cybersecurity governance, the people you invite to the table to make decisions with you as a team, and the time and space you dedicate to your day for important decision-making, instead of making those decisions ad hoc.

This is how I have seen it done best.

From my experience, there are three governing functions to consider as you build your security team. Keep in mind that for smaller teams, you may have a single group that owns all three functions. At larger organizations, each of these functions may be distinct. Either way, it is through these three functions that you can position your team to maximize influence inside the company.

1. Information Risk Council (IRC)
2. Security Leadership Team (SLT)
3. Initiative Review Board (IRB)

As we move through the following sections, don't worry about trying to memorize every role, description, and set of responsibilities. I am going to lay out the descriptions, typical members, and duties of the IRC, SLT, and IRB so you have the details handy when you need them later. As you read through this information, focus first on getting a general lay of the land—what the roles are, what they do, and why they're important. Then, bookmark this section and come back to it when it's time to start building your team.

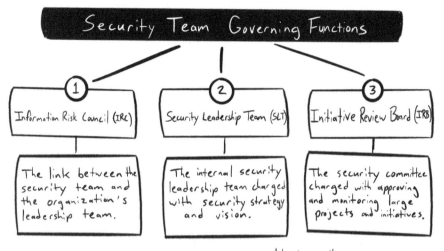

Security Team Governing Functions

1. Information Risk Council (IRC) — The link between the security team and the organization's leadership team.

2. Security Leadership Team (SLT) — The internal security leadership team charged with security strategy and vision.

3. Initiative Review Board (IRB) — The security committee charged with approving and monitoring large projects and initiatives.

For smaller security teams, this is likely all one team.
For larger security teams, it may be three separate teams.

Information Risk Council (IRC)

- **Description:** An information risk council (IRC) is the link between the security organization and leaders outside the security team. It is a cross-functional committee responsible for overseeing and managing information security risks across the organization. The IRC plays a crucial role in ensuring that information security practices align with business objectives, compliance requirements, and risk tolerance levels.

- **Typical owner:** The chief information security officer (CISO) or an equivalent senior executive often owns and chairs the IRC. This individual is responsible for the overall strategy, coordination, and reporting of information security risks to the organization's executive leadership and board of directors.

- **Common responsibilities:**

  - **Risk assessment and management:** The IRC is responsible for assessing information security risks across the organization. This involves identifying potential vulnerabilities and threats, evaluating their potential impact, and determining the likelihood of occurrence. The council then collaborates to prioritize and manage these risks effectively.

o **Policy and strategy development:** The IRC contributes to the development and maintenance of information security policies, standards, and guidelines, ensuring that these documents are aligned with industry best practices, regulatory requirements, and the organization's specific risk profile.

o **Risk appetite and tolerance:** Defining the organization's risk appetite and tolerance levels is a critical responsibility of the IRC. This involves determining how much risk the organization is willing to accept and what level of risk is unacceptable. These decisions guide risk management efforts.

o **Risk mitigation strategies:** The council discusses and approves risk mitigation strategies. This can involve recommending technical controls, process improvements, employee training, and other measures to reduce the organization's exposure to identified risks.

o **Incident response planning:** The IRC oversees the development and maintenance of incident response plans. This includes defining roles and responsibilities, establishing communication protocols, and conducting periodic tabletop exercises to ensure preparedness for potential security incidents.

o **Compliance and reporting:** Ensuring compliance with relevant laws, regulations, and industry standards is another responsibility of the IRC. The council reviews the organization's adherence to these requirements and prepares reports for executive leadership and relevant regulatory bodies.

o **Resource allocation:** The IRC assists in allocating resources for cybersecurity initiatives. This includes budget allocation for security tools, training, staffing, and other necessary resources to effectively manage information security risks.

o **Communication and awareness:** The council fosters a culture of cybersecurity awareness and education throughout the organization. It promotes the importance of security practices among employees, stakeholders, and partners.

o **Monitoring and review:** The IRC continually monitors the effectiveness of the organization's information security measures and risk management strategies. It ensures that controls are performing as intended and adjusts strategies as needed based on emerging threats and changes in the business environment.

o **Stakeholder collaboration:** The IRC facilitates collaboration between different departments, business units, and external partners to ensure that information security considerations are integrated into various aspects of the organization's operations.

Security Leadership Team (SLT)

- **Description:** The security leadership team (SLT) typically consists of the CISO and their direct reports. They are responsible for setting the overall cybersecurity strategy, vision, and objectives of the organization. The SLT plays a pivotal role in aligning cybersecurity initiatives with business goals and ensuring that the organization's digital assets are adequately protected.

- **Typical owner:** The chief information security officer (CISO) or equivalent senior cybersecurity executive typically owns and leads the SLT. The CISO reports to the organization's executive leadership or board of directors and is responsible for the overall security posture.

- **Common responsibilities:**

  o **Strategy and vision:** The SLT defines the organization's cybersecurity strategy and long-term vision. This involves identifying key security objectives, aligning them with business goals, and ensuring that security measures support the organization's growth and innovation.

  o **Resource allocation:** The team determines resource requirements for cybersecurity initiatives, including budget allocations, staffing needs, and technology investments. It ensures that the team has the necessary resources to implement the cybersecurity strategy effectively.

o **Collaboration and communication:** The SLT facilitates communication and collaboration between different departments and stakeholders. It educates executives, employees, and partners about the importance of cybersecurity and fosters a culture of security awareness.

o **Performance metrics and reporting:** The team establishes key performance indicators (KPIs) and metrics to measure the effectiveness of cybersecurity efforts. It prepares regular reports for executive leadership, demonstrating the impact of security measures and highlighting areas for improvement.

o **Talent development:** The SLT is responsible for building and nurturing a skilled cybersecurity workforce. This includes recruiting, training, and retaining cybersecurity professionals who can effectively address evolving threats.

o **Emerging technologies and trends:** The team stays informed about emerging cybersecurity technologies, threats, and industry trends. It evaluates their relevance to the organization and advises on their integration into the cybersecurity strategy.

Initiative Review Board (IRB)

- **Description:** An initiative review board (IRB) is a decision-making body responsible for assessing proposed cybersecurity initiatives and projects. The IRB ensures that these initiatives align with the organization's strategic goals, resource availability, and risk management strategies.

- **Typical owner:** The chief information security officer (CISO) or an equivalent senior cybersecurity leader typically owns and chairs the initiative review board. The CISO is responsible for ensuring that proposed initiatives align with the organization's security strategy and contribute to its overall security posture.

- **Common responsibilities:**

  o **Initiative assessment:** The IRB evaluates proposed cybersecurity initiatives, projects, and programs. It assesses their alignment with the organization's strategic objectives, risk tolerance, and resource availability.

o **Prioritization:** The board determines the priority of different initiatives based on factors such as potential impact, urgency, and alignment with the organization's risk appetite. This helps allocate resources effectively to the most critical security projects.

o **Resource allocation:** The IRB reviews and allocates resources, including budget, personnel, and technology, for approved initiatives. It ensures that adequate resources are available to support the successful execution of each project.

o **Business case review:** The IRB reviews the business cases for proposed initiatives, evaluating their expected benefits, costs, and return on investment. It ensures that the initiatives have a solid rationale and contribute to the organization's cybersecurity objectives.

o **Stakeholder engagement:** The IRB engages with stakeholders from various departments and business units to gather input and perspectives on proposed initiatives. This ensures that the initiatives address the needs of different parts of the organization.

o **Progress monitoring:** After approving initiatives, the board monitors their progress and performance. It reviews regular updates and milestones to ensure that projects are on track and delivering the expected outcomes.

o **Issue resolution:** If any issues or roadblocks arise during the execution of initiatives, the IRB provides guidance and support to address them. It may make decisions regarding changes in project scope, resource allocation, or risk management strategies.

o **Documentation and reporting:** The board maintains documentation related to the evaluation, decision-making process, and outcomes of each initiative. It prepares reports for executive leadership, showcasing the impact of security projects on the organization's security posture.

o **Lessons learned:** After initiatives are completed, the IRB conducts reviews to identify lessons learned and areas for improvement. This feedback informs the organization's approach to future cybersecurity projects.

At risk3sixty, we have helped hundreds of organizations implement governance structures just like the ones described above. It takes a lot of work and collaboration to get all of the right people at the table, but the results are worth the work. We have seen security teams go from siloed and marginalized to influential and top-of-mind with executives at the information risk council. We have seen teams frustrated by indecision become efficient evaluators of business cases in the initiative review board. The results are transformational. You just have to get started!

Security Team Operating Model: 6 Key Functions

Now that we have examined a few options for security governance, let's take a closer look at the six key functions of a security organization. From my experience, most security teams grow organically based on short-term need without a larger organizational design strategy. As a result, security teams often grow into inefficient, often bloated teams overindexed on a few skills, but underindexed on other skills needed to run the program. Ad hoc hiring just doesn't work in the long haul.

To avoid a misaligned team structure, every security team must think through the core functions required to run a successful program. Depending on the size and complexity of the security organization, sometimes each function is a distinct department with an entire team. For smaller organizations, a single individual may be responsible for multiple functions. Either way, whether your security function is a team of three hundred or a single individual, you will need to figure out a strategy to fulfill these functions.

But what are the functions of a high-performing security team? Good question.

In this section, we're going to remove some of that ambiguity so that you can start effectively defining key functions, establishing a common vocabulary, and devising roles and responsibilities in a way that makes sense to you and your organizational needs.

The following operating model is one of the more widely accepted models in the security business. I'm providing it as an example here to help you think about how to structure your team and approach the jobs within each category. Just like with the section above, you don't need to memorize this model; it's simply meant as a resource for you to adapt and apply, depending on how intentional and effective your current structure is. To help you plan your operating model, we've created a downloadable resource with all the functions already built out at: https://risk3sixty.com/stos

Security Team Operating Model

Information Risk Council	Security Leadership Team	Initiative Review Board

Office of the CISO	Detect & Respond	Governance Risk and Compliance	Product Security	Third Party Risk	Project Management	Shared Services

Function #1: Office of the CISO

- **Description:** This function is responsible for developing and implementing the overall security strategy and policies for the organization. It involves identifying security risks, defining security objectives, and ensuring alignment with business goals.

- **Typical owner:** Chief information security officer (CISO) or director of security.

- **Common responsibilities:** Developing security policies, security strategy and maturity roadmap, hiring, creating security awareness programs, managing security budgets, and providing security guidance to other departments.

Function #2: Detection and Response

- **Description:** This function focuses on monitoring, detecting, and responding to security incidents and threats. It involves utilizing various tools and technologies to identify potential security breaches and quickly respond to mitigate their impact.

- **Typical owner:** Security operations center (SOC) manager or incident response manager

- **Common responsibilities:** Setting up and managing security monitoring systems, analyzing security alerts and logs, investigating security incidents, coordinating incident response activities, conducting post-incident analysis and reporting, and continuously improving incident detection and response capabilities.

Function #3: Governance, Risk, and Compliance (GRC)

- **Description:** This function ensures that the organization complies with applicable laws, regulations, and industry standards. It involves assessing and managing risks, establishing and maintaining compliance frameworks, and monitoring the effectiveness of controls.

- **Typical owner:** Governance, risk, and compliance manager or compliance officer

- **Common responsibilities:** Developing and implementing risk management frameworks, conducting risk assessments and audits, monitoring compliance with relevant regulations, creating and maintaining compliance policies and procedures, coordinating internal and external audits, and providing guidance on compliance requirements.

Function #4: Product Security

- **Description:** This function focuses on securing the organization's products and services throughout their lifecycle, from design and development to deployment and maintenance. It involves integrating security into the product development process and ensuring the security of software and products.

- **Typical owner:** Product Security Manager or Application Security Manager

- **Common responsibilities:** Conducting security assessments and reviews of products and services, identifying and addressing security vulnerabilities, collaborating with development teams to implement secure coding practices, managing secure development lifecycle (SDLC) processes, providing security guidance to product teams, and coordinating product security incident response.

Function #5: Third-Party Risk

- **Description:** This function is responsible for assessing and managing the risks associated with the organization's relationships with third-party vendors, suppliers, and partners. It involves evaluating the security posture of third parties and ensuring their compliance with security requirements.

- **Typical owner:** Third-party risk manager or vendor risk manager.

- **Common responsibilities:** Developing and implementing third-party risk management programs, conducting due diligence assessments of third-party vendors, evaluating security controls and practices of third parties, negotiating and monitoring contractual security requirements, performing vendor security audits, and addressing any security risks or incidents related to third parties.

Function #6: Cybersecurity Project Management Office (PMO)

- **Description:** This function provides project management support and oversight for cybersecurity initiatives and programs within the organization. It involves coordinating and prioritizing cybersecurity projects, ensuring their successful execution, and tracking progress.

- **Typical owner:** Cybersecurity project manager or PMO director

- **Common responsibilities:** Defining project scope, objectives, and deliverables, developing project plans and schedules, allocating resources, coordinating project teams, tracking project progress and milestones, managing project budgets, communicating project status to stakeholders, and ensuring projects are completed within defined timelines and budgets.

Shared Responsibilities (IT, Legal, Engineering, HR)

- **Description:** This function involves collaboration and coordination with various departments across the organization to address cybersecurity requirements and ensure a holistic approach to security.

- **Typical owners:** Representatives from IT, legal, engineering, and HR departments.

- **Common responsibilities:** Collaborating with IT teams to implement security controls, ensuring legal compliance with privacy and data protection regulations, integrating security into engineering processes and product development, conducting security awareness training for employees, managing access controls and employee onboarding/offboarding procedures, and coordinating incident response efforts across departments.

Roles and Responsibilities for Each Function

Within each of these seven areas of competency are dozens of jobs and tasks that need to be accomplished. This is where most security leaders fail because they don't outline clear tasks to assigned owners and hold those owners accountable. The result is ambiguity, which breeds anxiety, erodes culture, and leads to a poorly operating security program.

Security leaders that take the important step of clarifying roles, assigning owners, and holding people accountable will transform their security team. People will be more enthusiastic about the work they do and work harder toward clear objectives. Dozens of people will work together like a symphony.

This might be the point where you roll your eyes. I can practically hear you asking, "Do you really expect me to go through the exercise of documenting a bunch of roles and responsibilities in a RACI chart?"

I said the same thing first time someone recommended it to me. What a huge administrative burden for such a small benefit! The whole suggestion sounded like nothing more than consultant-speak. And I hate those kinds of asks.

But I promise this tool is worth your time.

Getting clear about your operating model and the functions and roles within each function will provide so much clarity for the resources you need, skill and position gaps you have on your team, and so much more. If you do this exercise, you will suddenly realize that there are key roles that are completely vacant, that some of your team members are too busy, that some team members aren't busy enough, and that the root cause of some of your biggest process failures is that the role isn't assigned.

For example, take the "Office of the CISO" in the following graphic. That function has at least eleven unique roles and responsibilities that need to be clarified and assigned. This is also true for all six of the functions outlined in the previous section. That leaves a lot of opportunity for you to clarify expectations with your team.

Office of the CISO

This function is responsible for developing and implementing the overall security strategy and policies for the organization. It involves identifying security risks, defining security objectives, and ensuring alignment with business goals.

Role	R	A	C	I
Security Executive				
Report to the Board of Directors				
Information Risk Council Chair				
Security Strategy				
Designing Security Organizational Structure				
Security Program Budget				
Security Tooling and Software Selection				
Media and Public Relations				
Security Communications				
Security Awareness Training				
Managing Key Third Party and Consultant Relationships				

If you don't know where to begin, be sure to download the templates referenced in this chapter. We have done a lot of the heavy lifting for you when it comes to thinking about organizational design and common roles.

Communicating Roles to Owners

If you are like me, it might seem like roles are intuitive. I fall in the trap of believing that people should have a pretty good idea of what they are supposed to do. I don't need to tell them.

But that isn't the right way to think. And I have learned that the hard way many times.

This was a big problem for us at risk3sixty when we started promoting individual contributors to manager roles. I failed to realize that the title "manager" can be very intimidating and confusing. For example, when you promote someone to manager, what are they managing? Are they managing a function? People? Tasks? To solve that problem, we developed a new manager orientation program. The program formalized the way we communicate and clarified the manager role at our company.

Consider the same challenges on your team and clearly communicate your expectations to the individuals responsible for the success of each security function and role. Remember, this role is new to the person accepting it. Even if they have a good idea of the job they need to do, clarity will give them confidence and permission to execute it with confidence. Formally communicating their role is also a forcing mechanism to help ensure that you yourself have defined and communicate what you expect.

If you know what you expect of your team members, and they know what you expect of them, then that creates a powerful balance of freedom and accountability.

Write Good Job Descriptions

If you want to communicate roles to owners, you need good job descriptions. Please trust me when I say that writing job descriptions is going to feel like a lot of admin work. I get it. But if you want to make expectations clear, you have to do it.

Job descriptions provide a clear and consistent understanding of the roles and responsibilities associated with each position. They outline the key duties, tasks, and expectations for the role, ensuring that everyone has a shared understanding of what is required. Job descriptions formally define what you want and need from your team members and give you an important tool to hold them accountable.

One of the best examples of an effective job description I've ever seen is one produced by the City Bin in Dublin, Ireland. The City Bin is a trash collection company . . . a trash collection company that has won almost every award available in the category of best companies to work for.

This is an impressive feat. After all, trash collection isn't glamorous work. Even with their amazing company culture, the City Bin still grappled with high turnover rates and recruiting issues. The company paid well and treated its team members well, but at the end of the day, no one wanted to pick up trash.

That's when leadership at City Bin had an epiphany: switch the value proposition. Instead of focusing on trash collection, focus on a real benefit that comes with the job: physical fitness. City Bin looked at its primary demographic—specifically, young men—and realized that it offered something many young men wanted, especially aspiring athletes with dreams of making it in mixed martial arts.

So, the City Bin rewrote its job description to appeal to this group. The result, as you can see in the image, was pure brilliance:

The ad worked, and soon City Bin was swimming in applications from enthusiastic candidates excited at the chance to get paid to work out.

Now, as a security leader, it would be difficult for you to write a job description highlighting the benefits of physical fitness. But you get the idea. To write great job descriptions and attract great people, consider ways to look at your roles differently, to unearth overlooked benefits, and to hold new hires accountable for their success.

Owners Must Accept Responsibility

A few years ago, risk3sixty lost an extremely high-performing employee, who we'll call Geoff, because we failed to properly set expectations with him. I saw him as a shoo-in for a management role, and when I offered him the position, he leapt at it.

Then, a couple of months later, he left the company for another opportunity.

I was shocked. This wasn't the outcome I'd expected. And later, I learned that it wasn't the outcome Geoff had expected either.

So, what happened? As Geoff later shared with me, he had been excited about the opportunity, but once he stepped into his new role, he felt an overwhelming sense of ambiguity around his responsibilities.

This was my fault. When I offered Geoff the management role, I never bothered to provide a detailed job description, cover specific expectations, or discuss how his workload would change. I simply assumed he understood the role and the responsibilities, congratulated him on the promotion, and sent him on his way.

My heart was in the right place. I believed in Geoff and trusted him so much that I didn't think I needed to follow a special process. However, because I failed to provide him with the support he needed to hit the ground running, Geoff began feeling a tremendous sense of pressure and anxiety.

In reality, he was doing a pretty good job onboarding himself, but he didn't know it. In fact, he was certain he was failing—causing him to regularly lose sleep over his perceived shortcomings.

Meanwhile, I was clueless. I didn't know he was struggling emotionally. I didn't know he felt unsupported. All I saw were the results, which were strong. Eventually, the stress and uncertainty became too much, and Geoff decided he would rather take a role with more structure and certainty somewhere else than struggle in ambiguity with us.

I was lucky Geoff eventually shared this with me, even if it was too late to keep him at the company. First, it gave me a chance to apologize for putting him in that situation. Second, it gave me the opportunity to completely revisit how we handled promotions at the company so that we wouldn't lose good people like Geoff again.

Here's what we do now whenever a team member is in line for a new promotion:

1. I present a job description, explain it to them, and highlight why the new role is important.
2. We talk about how the role differs from their current responsibilities, how it supports the business, and the methods of accountability in place.
3. I communicate my expectations for their success and give them a chance to share their expectations and questions.

That may sound standard, but we weren't doing any of that before, and it cost us good people.

After I have made the offer and discussed expectations, I make it clear to the team member that they own their decision and that they're free to make whatever choice is best for them. To do that, I'll say, "If you don't want this job—because this is really the first time we've talked at length about it—please know that you don't have to accept it. You can continue doing what you're doing, and you'll be valuable. Either way, I want you here. Sit on it, think about it, and then come back to me in a couple of days to tell me whether you're formally accepting the offer."

Typically, team members will respond immediately by saying they want the job. I thank them for their enthusiasm and congratulate them on their achievement. After all, a promotion offer is a meaningful step in anyone's career, and I want them to recognize that they've earned it.

But I still ask them to sleep on it. I am sincere in giving every team member a choice, and I want them to have the confidence and certainty in their decision that can only come with meaningful reflection. That way, they will fully own their decision—and have no excuse for not following through.

Risk3sixty has followed this process for a few years now, and as a result, we've had much greater success with promoting our A players. We've found that this approach both addresses a practical issue of clarity and offers a way to make a bigger, more ceremonial deal of the change. While this approach never would have dawned on me if not for Geoff, just a few small tweaks have made a world of difference in our success.

Establishing Key Performance Indicators (KPIs)
for Each Role

Chris is an exceptional leader. In a meeting one day, he caught me off guard with a question:

"How do I know if I am winning?"

That was his clever way of asking for key performance indicators for his role. What measurables indicated that he was doing his job well? I didn't have an answer at the time, but ever since, I have made it a habit to be able to tell my team how to measure their own performance through key performance indicators—commonly known as KPIs.

KPIs have several benefits, whether for the team member, the team leader, the team itself, or the organization at large:

- **For the team member:** KPIs outline specific goals, targets, and performance benchmarks so they can prioritize and align their efforts.

- **For the team leader:** KPIs allow leaders to objectively measure an employee's progress and achievements. Regular performance evaluations on these KPIs provide feedback, identify areas for improvement, and recognize outstanding performance.

- **For the team:** Clearly defined KPIs provide a common language for discussing performance and progress within the team, encouraging open discussions about goals, challenges, and opportunities for support.

- **For the organization:** KPIs help team members understand how their contributions impact the broader goals of the team and the company, fostering a sense of purpose and enabling employees to prioritize their work effectively.

More than anything, KPIs provide the team members with a clear target to help them know whether, in Chris's words, they're winning. Clear and measurable KPIs provide employees with a sense of direction and purpose, milestones and targets to strive for, and a common language for discussing performance, progress, and opportunities for support or resources.

To begin setting KPIs for your security team, keep it simple. Set one to three KPIs for every role—and no more.

Don't Say I Didn't Warn You

All right, I'm going to be honest with you. I'm nervous about this chapter. I'm nervous because the recommendations in this chapter are the type of recommendations that people tend to ignore.

Why?

Because you have a job to do. You have urgent tasks, people issues, board meetings, and fires to put out. And designing an organization takes deep thinking, a lot of collaboration, and extraordinary patience. But I promise that if you take organizational design seriously, it will revolutionize your security program.

So, you have a decision to make.

You can do nothing. In this case, you will have to live with a few things. You can live in an organization where you are marginalized. You can continue to be cynical because you don't have a seat at the table. You live in a world where you can't justify your headcount. You can live in a world where you don't own your budget. This is a bleak outlook.

Or you can put in the work to control your destiny by clarifying your team's roles. In this world, you will position yourself as a person of influence inside your company. You will empower your team to make better decisions about which roles you need in order to best meet your security objectives. You will have confidence in your hiring plan and your budget. You will have dedicated time and space for your team to make important decisions. And the result will be a high-performing and well-respected security team.

Which future do you want?

As a leader, it's your job to initiate this work—and if you're like most security leaders out there, it's one of the biggest gaps that you didn't even know you had. If, after all this, you choose not to dedicate the time and mental energy to do this step right, well, don't say I didn't warn you.

But if you are reading this book, I know you have what it takes.

You've got this!

Download the Tools

Download the tools referenced in this chapter to document your team's Roles at www.risk3sixty.com/stos

Download it
by scanning this
(you won't
regret it)

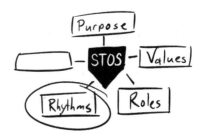

CHAPTER 5

RHYTHMS

Executive Summary

Leaders make sure everyone is on the same page. In this chapter, we will explore how leaders can establish processes to provide the right data at the right time to the right people to inform decision-making. We will explore example meeting agendas and cadences that facilitate effective information sharing and communication. We will cover real-world examples you can pull inspiration from as you consider the rhythms and cadences that make sense for your team.

Self-Assessment Questions

☐	Do you have a documented annual calendar?
☐	How does your team share data and information across the team?
☐	Do you have a formalized annual planning process?
☐	Does your team have productive meetings?
☐	Do you have documented and shared KPIs for your security team?

Why Rhythms Matter

Communication is a funny thing. Anyone who has been married or has kids knows how hard it is. And communication gets harder and more complex the more people involved.

At risk3sixty, I have watched communication become increasingly complex over the years. It used to be just me. Then me and a business partner. Now it is me, my business partner, six executives, over fifty team members, and hundreds of clients. If you do the math, that creates a lot of possible communication pathways.

The bottom line is that communication is hard. You have to do it clearly and do it often.

That is why rhythms are so important.

Rhythms create predictable cadences for teams. Predictability creates confidence. Confidence allows team members to focus on doing their best work, knowing that the right information will be provided at the right time.

Rhythms are made up of the regular set of meetings and data shared by the organization to keep everyone on the same page.

Rhythms create harmony.

I remember when our team at risk3sixty hit about fifty people. That is when communication started to get complicated. For one, it wasn't up to me to communicate everything anymore. I would communicate to directors, who communicated to managers, who communicated to staff. That is three levels of communication and three opportunities for things to get mistranslated and misinterpreted—which is exactly what happened.

At first, these communication mishaps created a lot of frustration for our team. The loss of information led to feelings of loss of control. Loss of control led to insecurity. And insecurity led to loss of trust.

And that is a very big deal.

It all came to a head when we had an extended leadership off-site meeting. One of our directors, a close colleague, decided to be vulnerable: "We are losing trust in the executive leadership team."

That news hit us hard.

Over the next few months, we worked hard on communication. We overhauled all of our rhythms to get to the next level. We implemented new governance structures and reports for data sharing, upgraded meeting cadences, documented everything, and then retrained the whole team.

I see this same pattern with security teams.

As security teams grow, they lose touch both with each other and with the business. They get out of sync with business objectives. They stop communicating between business units, product teams, and functional areas. And left unattended, really bad things start to happen. Goals are missed, people start to quit, and the security team fails to protect the organization like they are committed to.

This is precisely the challenge we saw with one client, whom we'll call Cloud Technology Company (CTM). The board of directors was driving some efficiency and cost-cutting measures, not through layoffs, but rather through evaluating and streamlining processes. One way they decided to streamline was by making security a corporate function rather than dedicating a distinct, decentralized security team to every product, which led to siloed processes, underutilized staff, and tool duplication.

For this large reorg initiative, the CISO was prepared to make decisions quickly. While the reasoning was sound, essentially everyone below the CISO, including the managers and staff, felt cynical and disheartened. They didn't think the changes made sense, and they weren't invested.

As we dug deeper, we realized no one understood *why* the changes were happening. To them, the reorg seemed like just another instance of corporate coming in and ordering them around without thinking through the implications. Some of them even thought layoffs were coming.

It became clear the security team had no process to disseminate information up and down the organization. So, we worked with the CISO to establish rhythms, create a cross-departmental information risk council, and establish an annual off-site to discuss new objectives and get the team on board. Then, we organized quarterly check-ins for the whole team to receive progress updates and hone any strategy points.

A year after they had begun implementing these changes, CTM found that team morale was at an all-time high. When people have a clear understanding of why a decision was made, how leadership arrived at it using sound logic with the best interest of the business in mind, how it will impact them, and what they need to do about it, they trust the process and get on board. This intentional approach to communication corrected their previous problems and allowed the organization to pull off some big changes. The secret had nothing to do with finances or staff capabilities; it was purely about information dissemination.

To manage change successfully, you have to talk about it.

Failure to communicate well often leads to failure to achieve your goal. It sounds simple, but this principle gets overlooked to the detriment of many companies.

In this chapter, I will share some of the lessons I have learned about upgrading your team's rhythms so that everyone is on the same page and operating as a synchronized unit. I am going to share with you the governance structure I have seen work, the specific meetings you can consider, and even meeting agendas. I hope you can take this information and use it as inspiration to solve some of the challenges you may be facing at your own organization.

Security Program Rhythms

Your meeting cadences should form the heartbeat of your business. If done correctly, the right cadence will create natural stopping points to share data, make decisions, and provide updates to your team. Great meeting cadences will promote data sharing, reduce ad hoc meetings, and get everyone on the same page and rowing in the same direction.

In the following sections, I'll share a common set of meeting rhythms and the types of data you can share at each. Remember, you do not need to memorize this information. Use this chapter to draw inspiration for your own set of rhythms tailored to the needs of your team.

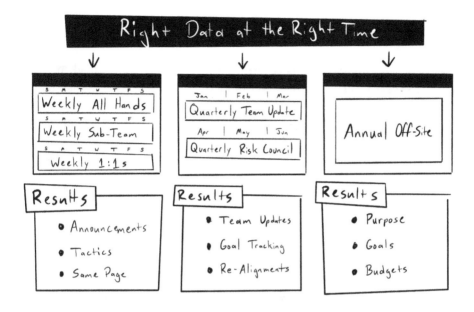

Note: If you want a quick, easy-to-reference copy of the meeting agendas that follow, you can download an example meeting agenda for each of these rhythms at https://risk3sixty.com/stos

Annual Team Off-Site

The annual team meeting is an opportunity to celebrate wins, create transparency around where your team is headed and why, and get everyone focused on the future. As a result, these meetings enable your team to evaluate the organization's strategy, provide feedback, and buy into the vision. This helps to ensure that everyone is aligned with the organization's mission and goals and provides an opportunity to make any necessary adjustments to the strategy to reflect changes in the business environment.

On an individual level, the annual planning meeting helps your team to prioritize initiatives, projects, and goals. This empowers team members to self-manage and allocate resources more effectively and avoid wasting time and money on lower-priority initiatives. It provides an opportunity to establish clear targets and deadlines, which leads to better accountability for performance, and ensures that everyone is working toward the same goals.

Part of a good annual meeting is ceremonial. Annual off-sites provide a break from the normal office routine and can help team members focus on strategy rather than day-to-day routines. Further, being in a different location stimulates fresh thinking, inspires creativity, and promotes a sense of unity among team members. Even the act of scheduling the meeting itself provides team members with dedicated time and space to think strategically and get on the same page.

From a leadership perspective, annual meetings provide a forum for clear and effective communication. Team members can discuss important issues face-to-face, ask questions, and receive feedback in a collaborative and supportive environment. This is a time to make your vision clear and get everyone excited about what the team plans to accomplish.

One of the most famous off-site organizers was Apple cofounder Steve Jobs, who famously organized an annual top-secret "Top 100" management off-site at the company.

From: Steve Jobs ◀▮▮▮▮▮▮▮▮
Subject: **Top 100 - A**
Date: October 24, 2010 6:12:41 PM PDT
To: ET▮▮▮▮▮▮▮▮▮▮▮

Here's my current cut.

Steve

1. 2011 Strategy - SJ
   - who are we?
     - headcount, average age, ...
     - VP count, senior promotions in last year
     - percent new membership at this meeting
   - what do we do?
     - pie chart of units/product line and revenues/product line
     - same charts with tablets + phones merged together
   - Post PC era
     - Apple is the first company to get here
     - Post PC products now 66% of our revenues
     - iPad outsold Mac within 6 months
     - Post PC era = more mobile (smaller, thinner, lighter) + communications + apps + cloud services
   - 2011: Holy War with Google
     - all the ways we will compete with them
     - primary reason for this Top 100 meeting - you will hear about what we're doing in each presentation
   - 2011: Year of the Cloud
     - we invented Digital Hub concept
       - PC as hub for all your digital assets - contacts, calendars, bookmarks, photos, music, videos
     - digital hub (center of our universe) is moving from PC to cloud
       - PC now just another client alongside iPhone, iPad, iPod touch, ...
       - Apple is in danger of hanging on to old paradigm too long (innovator's dilemma)
       - Google and Microsoft are further along on the technology, but haven't quite figured it out yet
     - tie all of our products together, so we further lock customers into our ecosystem
   - 2015: new campus

2. State of the Company - Peter & Tim
   - FY2010 recap
   - FY2011 plan
   - where is our business - geo analysis (NA, Euro, Japan, Asia, possibly break out china) (present on map)
   - key milestones, trends & future goals
   - comparisons with Google, Samsung, HTC, Motorola & RIM

3. iPhone - Joz & Bob
   - 2011 Strategy:
     - "plus" iPhone 4 with better antenna, processor, camera & software to stay ahead of competitors until mid 2012
     - have LTE version in mid 2012
     - create low cost iPhone model based on iPod touch to replace 3GS
   - Business & competitive update
     - show Droid and RIM ads
   - Verizon iPhone
     - schedule, marketing, ...
   - iPhone 5 hardware
     - H4 performance
     - new antenna design, etc
     - new camera
     - schedule
   - iPhone nano plan
     - cost goal
     - show model (and/or renderings) - Jony

Excerpt of a leaked agenda from Apple's Top 100 Meeting.[17]

---

[17] Twitter. @TechEmails. August 19, 2021.
https://twitter.com/TechEmails/status/1428400060019068933?s=20

The meeting was so secret it wasn't known outside the company until documents leaked due to a lawsuit with Samsung and an email outlining the agenda of this specific Top 100 meeting became public in 2014. Attendees were asked not to put the meeting on their calendars and weren't even allowed to drive to the location themselves. From the team's perspective, the meeting was sacred. Members were forced to take it seriously and arrive ready to get to work. In that way, the meeting was optimized for results.

During the elaborately staged two-to-three-day day off-site meeting, Jobs and his chief lieutenants would discuss strategy, communicate Apple's vision, and get the team excited about the future. That was the power of Steve Jobs and a well-produced annual off-site meeting.

Your annual offsites don't need to be as dramatic and secretive as Apple's. That said, these meetings are important, so carve out the time for them every year and conduct them with a degree of decorum and intentionality.

I've seen many security teams take this approach to great effect.

For instance, in Chapter 2 I introduced you to Stacy, who successfully transformed her vulnerability management program across four business units to save her company $10 million. This success sparked a new commitment within the company to formalize their rhythms. "After our success with the vulnerability management program, I knew that we had to formalize our approach to getting the whole team on the same page about our goals." As a result, Stacy said, "We decided to start hosting an annual kick-off meeting. We invite team members from all over the country and use the event to roll out the year's strategy."

The effort paid off.

"We are committed to socializing organizational change, informing team members of new initiatives, and giving them a forum to ask questions. As a result, everyone leaves the offsite fired up and ready to dig in." Stacy told me.

Here is a template meeting agenda you can use for your own off-site meeting:

Annual Off-Site Agenda

<u>**Purpose**</u>

The purpose of this meeting is to cast a vision for next year for the security team in alignment with business objectives.

<u>**Attendees**</u>

All team members

<u>**Duration**</u>

Half- to full-day

<u>**Preparation Checklist**</u>

- Speak with the executive team to clearly understand the business's top-level company objectives. Ensure that security projects are clearly mapped to the business's objectives.
- Review the results of audits, penetration tests, and risk assessment activities. Allow these inputs to inform your plan for next year.
- Inventory top projects for next year based on your judgment. Seek to obtain buy-in from the executive team.
- Develop a resource plan and have it approved (e.g., budget, hiring plan, toolset needs).
- Ensure all security program maintenance activities are scheduled (e.g., security audits, penetration tests, BCP/DR tests, policy refresh, etc.).
- Review and update your STOS.
- Book an off-site location.
- Prepare and print out any meeting materials for the team.

Annual Off-Site Agenda (Continued)

Agenda

Review Vision, Mission, and Core Values

Review the security team's vision, mission, and core values. Use this as a culture-building moment. Consider telling stories, sharing team photos, or giving shout-outs to people who demonstrated these core values, and talk about how security made a positive impact on the business or industry. Get creative!

Where We've Been

- Highlight new team members and their contributions.
- Highlight key accomplishments of the security team and company.
- Review goals to actuals.

Where We're Going

- Review company goals.
- Review security team goals and how those goals will support company goals.
- Review the key projects and initiatives for next year.
- Review planned schedule for next year.
- Review the Security Team Operating System.

Goal Setting and Team Review

Give your team time to set goals and key objectives for themselves for the next quarter. Use the SMART format for all goals. Each of your team members will report progress toward goals each week and at the quarterly meeting.

Something Fun

Do something fun. It could be a team dinner, happy hour, bowling, or anything else you might enjoy. This is for team building and showing appreciation for everyone's hard work.

Quarterly Team Review

Sometimes, three months can seem like a year. There is a phenomenon in business—I swear it is a law of business physics—where a team needs to be reminded of what is important every ninety days. Otherwise, things start to get off track, and people get distracted. The quarterly team meeting is an opportunity to refocus and reenergize the whole team around your vision and goals.

Quarterly meetings are also an important accountability check-in. They create a dedicated time and space to review where you have been and the commitments you've made, and then to report on progress toward those commitments. When people know they are responsible for reporting to the whole team, they feel a greater sense of urgency to make progress.

Most importantly, quarterly meetings are an opportunity for teams to come together. Successful teams are built on strong relationships and trust. Quarterly team meetings offer an opportunity for team members to connect on a personal level and foster that camaraderie and trust. Through team-building activities, sharing success stories, and recognizing individual contributions, these meetings cultivate a sense of belonging. When trust is established, collaboration flourishes, and team members feel empowered to take risks and contribute their best work.

At risk3sixty, we've found there's a need to manage the energy of business teams over the course of a year. People get energized at the annual kickoff and feel ready to go, but their energy starts to flag around the three-month mark. They've been in the trenches, haven't talked to everyone, and haven't broken bread together in quite a while.

Seeing this flagging energy, we committed to hosting quarterly offsites in our Atlanta office. Because we're a hybrid company—about half our team works in Atlanta and half our team elsewhere—this means flying a bunch of people out every three months at our expense. Of course, we see tremendous value in these face-to-face meetups, so we're more than happy to do that.

At our quarterly meetings, we review the goals we set at the annual kickoff, discuss our progress, and make adjustments so our teams can enter the next quarter feeling energized and ready to go. To further build that energy, we hand out some swag, show a hype video, and celebrate being in each other's company.

Remember, we're not machines. We are human beings who have emotional needs. Strategy is important, but so is your team's energy and emotional state as they implement your strategy. Otherwise, what's the point?

Quarterly Team Update Agenda

<u>Purpose</u>

The purpose of this meeting is to discuss progress toward the annual plan, any changes, and plans for the next quarter.

<u>Attendees</u>

All team members

<u>Duration</u>

Half-day (including team event)

<u>Preparation Checklist</u>

Speak with the executive team to clearly understand the business's top-level company objectives. Ensure that security projects are clearly mapped to the business's objectives.

- Review the result of security KPIs, audits, penetration tests, and risk assessment activities that were completed in the last quarter. Allow these inputs to inform your next quarter.
- Review the status of top projects currently complete or in progress.
- Review the resource plan (e.g., budget, hiring plan, toolset needs).
- Review any business-level updates, such as annual reports, recent strategic initiatives, etc., that may impact your security strategy.
- Review and update your Management Operating System.
- Prepare and print out any meeting materials for the team.

Quarterly Team Update Agenda (Continued)

Agenda

Review Vision, Mission, and Core Values

Review the security team's vision, mission, and core values. Use this as a culture-building moment. Consider telling stories, sharing team photos, or giving shout-outs to people who demonstrated these core values, and talk about how security made a positive impact on the business or industry. Get creative!

Where We've Been

- Highlight new team members and their contributions.
- Highlight key accomplishments of the security team and company.
- Review any lessons learned (e.g., audit results, team member feedback, etc.).
- Review goals to actuals.

Where We're Going

- Review company goals.
- Review security team goals and how those goals will support company goals.
- Review the key projects and initiatives for next quarter.
- Review planned schedule for next quarter.
- Review the Security Team Operating System.

Goal Setting and Team Review

Give your team time to set goals and key objectives for themselves for the next quarter. Use the SMART format for all goals. Each of your team members will report progress toward goals each week and at the quarterly meeting.

Something Fun

Do something fun. It could be a team dinner, happy hour, bowling, or anything else you might enjoy. This is for team building and showing appreciation for everyone's hard work.

Quarterly Information Risk Council (IRC)

If you want authority and influence in your company, establish an IRC (see Chapter 4). The IRC provides an opportunity for you to build relationships with stakeholders across the organization. This includes representatives from IT, legal, finance, and other departments.

The IRC can help you drive change within the organization by identifying and prioritizing information risks and recommending appropriate risk mitigation strategies. It also provides an opportunity to collaborate with other stakeholders to influence decisions related to investments in cybersecurity, compliance with relevant regulations, and other critical decisions related to information security.

But from my experience, the IRC is only as effective as the meeting cadence that supports it.

One CISO I know, John, runs his IRC meetings extremely well. In fact, he's one of the few CISOs I've seen who's able to get members of the C-suite to not only attend these IRC meetings, but attend them *regularly* and be engaged the whole time.

This is no small feat. For most security teams, executive attendance at IRC meetings goes something like this: the executive attends the first one but doesn't understand the value. Then, the executive might come to the second one, but they're disengaged and rarely speak. By the third meeting, the executive is dialing in remotely with the camera off, and by the fourth one, they're a no-show. As a result, the meetings lose purpose and fizzle out.

Not at John's IRC meetings. John comes prepared, starting with the little things to help people feel comfortable, such as coffee or breakfast. Next, John focuses on recognition. If the CTO or CFO is in attendance, for instance, he'll be ready with shout-outs for their team, highlighting their accomplishments and why they matter. Instead of just being one more demand on a busy executive's schedule, the meeting becomes an opportunity for C-suite participants to look good in front of their peers.

John also has another secret weapon that he's always ready to deploy: the meeting before the meeting. John meets with his CFO and CTO ahead of time to see whether they have any messages they'd like him to relay and to give them a quick overview of what to expect. If he needs them to make a decision related to an item on the meeting agenda, he gives them a heads-up, along with the background information they need to make that decision. This helps John to avoid the appearance of "gotcha" moments, where the executive might feel called out on the floor unfairly and without any warning.

Through these meetings-before-the-meeting, John is able to scaffold the information-sharing and decision-making process so that his executives can be as effective as possible and come out looking like champions. As a result, those C-suite members not only happily attend, but become his cheerleaders as well. They have his back and support him—and rarely throw up any roadblocks.

John offers a great example of how to design IRC meetings that are highly engaging, drive important decisions, and build rapport between department leaders. And because of all the careful cultural work that John puts in before, during, and in between his meetings, his security team has an outsized influence within the organization.

Here is how to structure your IRC meeting agenda so you can be as successful as John:

Quarterly IRC Agenda

Purpose

The purpose of this meeting is to meet with members of the executive team to discuss the security and compliance program.

Attendees

Members of the IRC

Duration

1 hour

Preparation Checklist

- Speak with the executive team to clearly understand the business's top-level company objectives. Ensure that security projects are clearly mapped to the business's objectives.

Quarterly IRC Agenda (Continued)

- Meet with members of the executive team to understand top priorities and what information they need from the meeting.
- Review the results of audits, penetration tests, and risk assessment activities that were completed the last quarter. Allow these inputs to inform your summary to the executive team.
- Review the status of top projects currently complete or in progress.
- Review the resource plan (e.g., budget, hiring plan, toolset needs).
- Review all security program maintenance activities (e.g., security audits, penetration test, BCP/DR tests, policy refresh, etc.).
- Prepare and print out any meeting materials for the team.

Meeting Agenda

Executive Summary

This section is designed as an executive summary:

- Where we have been the last quarter
- Risk heat map
- Key initiatives in progress
- Next quarter in focus
- Questions from executives

Security and Compliance Program Updates

This section is designed to provide more detail on important initiatives:

- Security initiative summary and status

Program Key Performance Indicators

- Summary of program KPIs (will only cover issues, otherwise this is for visibility only).

Quarterly Initiative Review Board (IRB) Meeting

An Initiative Review Board (IRB) is a crucial organizational structure within a company's cybersecurity framework, overseen by the CISO or a designated senior leader. The IRB serves as a governance body responsible for evaluating, prioritizing, and approving proposed cybersecurity initiatives and projects. It plays a pivotal role in ensuring that the organization's strategic objectives align with its cybersecurity efforts while managing risks effectively. The IRB is composed of key stakeholders from various departments, including IT, legal, compliance, and business units, to provide a holistic perspective on the potential impacts and benefits of proposed initiatives.

IRBs help address the dynamic and complex nature of cybersecurity by providing a structured place to review and approve projects and initiatives. This ensures that proposed initiatives receive a thorough evaluation that considers their alignment with the organization's overall cybersecurity strategy, compliance requirements, resource allocation, and potential risks. This central oversight helps prevent ad hoc implementation of security solutions and minimizes the possibility of misaligned projects that could lead to inefficiencies, wasted resources, or security gaps. By fostering collaboration among diverse stakeholders, the IRB enhances transparency, accountability, and communication throughout the organization's cybersecurity endeavors.

Put another way, big organizations tend to have many different teams that want to do stuff, but they get stalled because there's no place to get approval, to decide if a plan is even a good idea, or to get budget allocated for it—even if the ask is small, such as a $2,500 project management tool. Businesses without an IRB have no dedicated place to review requests and business cases. As a result, the decisions either stall out or get made in a silo—which leads to duplication, confusion, or failure. Over time, organizations tend to build a whole backlog of pending decisions, with no clear path to resolution. So, with chronic obstacles and bureaucracy holding them up, team members become unable to do their jobs effectively.

One CIO I know, Kevin, created an IRB at his company precisely to eradicate this decision limbo. Along with setting aside dedicated time and space to surface issues and make decisions, Kevin created a one-page format for team members to bring a problem to the table and talk about it. Ahead of the IRB meeting, everyone submits any IRB topics to the chair, who then reviews each request and sorts what's ready to discuss from what isn't a good fit or needs more information to proceed. Then, at the meeting, the team then discusses as many of the submissions as they can in the allotted time.

Kevin's first two IRB meetings were almost overwhelming, with too many decisions to make in too little time. By the fourth or fifth meeting, though, they had worked through the backlog and only had one decision to discuss.

There's a twist to this story. While Kevin used to run these IRBs for another organization, now he runs them for us—and I can say from firsthand experience that the difference has been night and day. Once we had a process to track and make decisions on all the issues that had been floating around, we realized how much value these meetings offered. Perhaps more importantly, these meetings freed up time, eliminating the need for ad hoc conversations on Slack and spur-of-the-moment choices just because someone happened to bring something up in conversation.

With the IRB template, we could capture the situation, get more information as needed, put it on the agenda, and make a structured decision. Here's how we did it:

Quarterly IRB Agenda
Purpose The IRB serves as a governance body responsible for evaluating, prioritizing, and approving proposed cybersecurity initiatives and projects. **Attendees** Members of the IRB **Duration** 1 hour **Preparation Checklist** • All team members to submit initiatives for review and approval at least one week in advance of the meeting.

Quarterly IRB Agenda (Continued)

- Submitted initiatives should be in an approved template and meet defined thresholds to be considered for evaluation.
- All team members review submitted initiatives to prepare questions in advance.

Meeting Agenda

- Review submitted IRB.
- Questions and comments on initiative.
- Approve, deny, or request more information on submitted initiative.

Weekly All-Hands Meeting

The purpose of a weekly all-hands meeting is to bring together the whole team to discuss key updates. These meetings typically occur on a regular basis— usually weekly, as the name implies—and serve as a forum for team members to share information, collaborate, and stay aligned.

Does a weekly cadence sound like overkill? Maybe, but consider the alternative. I've seen some security teams go years without receiving any sort of meaningful update—all because they didn't have a structured communication plan in place. It's easy for people to get caught in the whirlwind of their own jobs, losing sight of the bigger organizational picture.

Viewed in that light, a weekly, thirty-minute (or less) all-hands meeting can do wonders for sharing updates, celebrating wins, shouting out excellent work from team members, and otherwise getting everyone on the same page.

I stole this idea from the CEO of a healthcare payments company named Thomas Blick, who was a client of ours. He's a fantastic guy, a gentle giant, standing six feet seven inches tall. His company had a break room where they built a low-budget, five-by-five "stage" with a modest presentation monitor behind it and an at-home karaoke-grade PA system to power the presentations. The stage wasn't much—it was essentially made of two-by-fours elevated just above the ground—but it was just enough to create a physical space and a sense of atmosphere for these meetings. Oh, and of course there was coffee too.

Each week, everyone knew what to expect: a different team member would get on the stage and present, there would be some social bonding, and then there would be some substantive updates on the state of the company. Everyone at the company would leave knowing what was going on, what was important for the week, and how they were tracking relative to their goals.

I have seen teams do these meeting in person and remote—so format is less important. Each configuration is a little different and unique to the company culture and team, but the bottom line is it harnesses human energy and gets people through the ebbs and flows.

By establishing the weekly cadence and ensuring everyone has updates and gets wins to celebrate, no one gets too far off track, and everyone has important context about where the organization is and what to expect so they're not just reacting to fires. The culture continues to strengthen over time, because everyone has a regular opportunity to reflect on who they are as a team, what they've done, and where they're going.

Weekly All Hands Agenda

Purpose

The purpose of this meeting is to establish a cadence to keep everyone on the team in alignment.

Attendees

All team members

Duration

25 minutes

Agenda

- Values and performance callouts for individual team members.

Weekly All Hands Agenda (Continued)

- Important announcements.
- Goals and objectives scorecard.
- Rotational sub-team update.
  a. On a rotational basis, each sub-team is given ten minutes to provide an update on objectives, accomplishments, progress toward goals, or other information relevant to the larger group.

Weekly Sub-Team Standup

Sub-team meetings are integral components of effective organizational communication and collaboration. For a CISO overseeing multiple teams, such as the Governance, Risk, and Compliance (GRC) team and the Detect and Response team, these sub-team meetings serve as focused opportunities for each specialized group to discuss specific matters related to their domain. These meetings typically involve smaller groups of team members who share expertise and responsibilities in a particular area, allowing for in-depth discussions, problem-solving, and knowledge sharing.

These weekly sub-team standups can apply to the needs of any sub-team. For instance:

- At a GRC team sub-team meeting, topics could include discussions on upcoming regulatory changes, compliance assessments, and risk assessment methodologies. The team members might review the organization's adherence to industry standards, evaluate potential vulnerabilities in business processes, and strategize ways to improve overall governance.

- A Detect and Response team sub-team meeting might cover topics related to threat intelligence, incident response tactics, and the analysis of recent security incidents. The team could discuss emerging cyber threats, review incident trends, share insights gained from ongoing investigations, and collaborate on refining incident response procedures.

My favorite example of the value of weekly sub-team standups, however, comes from within our own company. At risk3sixty, all of our practice leaders (our top-level managers) are required to have a weekly one-on-one with their direct reports and a weekly team meeting at the sub-practice level.

In essence, each of these practice leaders is functionally running a small business. Once we have defined the business objective and how a department will support that business objective, it is the practice leader's responsibility to determine how the team will meet those objectives within the context of their jobs.

At first, these sub-team standups can feel like just another meeting in an already crowded schedule and workload. However, our managers often find these meetings actually ease their workload rather than add to it.

Sawyer, one of our practice leaders, has helped the rest of the company see the true potential of these sub-team standups. In fact, his approach has informed the way we work elsewhere in the business and how we coach some of our clients.

Here's how he does it. First, he creates a slide deck called "High-Impact Commitments." During the weekly meetings, Sawyer reminds the team of the big-picture objectives that they're trying to accomplish, and he gets each team member to make a high-impact commitment for that week, something outside their normal work. Maybe they'll commit to finishing a template, or having a hard conversation, or developing a piece of thought leadership—whatever might apply to the most important goal the team is trying to accomplish at the time. Then he catalogs those commitments live, each week.

The next week, they'll run through the team's status on those commitments—done, in progress, or still to do—which usually only takes about five minutes. Then, the team members who have completed their big-picture objective will commit to a new one.

Because these commitments help move the needle the most for the company, they comprise the bulk of the meeting time. The rest of the time is spent on quick updates, announcements, and shout-outs.

Sawyer tracks these commitments, and, at the end of the year, he looks back over the previous fifty-two weeks as way of measuring his team's progress. The results are incredibly inspiring, providing concrete data of how much everyone has achieved—and in turn, making performance reviews a breeze.

With this system, Sawyer has all the information he needs to celebrate each team member's success, create a sense of momentum, and get the team fired up. Most importantly, this system helps team members to understand how they're contributing to a larger strategy, providing both short-term and long-term motivation.

Weekly Team Stand-Up Agenda

<u>Purpose</u>

The purpose of this meeting is to review and prioritize top priorities for core teams or sub-teams.

<u>Attendees</u>

Sub-team members

<u>Duration</u>

15-30 minutes

<u>Agenda</u>

- Good news and announcements.
- Sub-team scorecard.
- Individual status.
    - o Did you do what you said you would do last week?
    - o What are you doing this week?
    - o Any barriers to success?

- Status of big-picture team goals
    - o Present, on-track, or off-track status for each major goal.
    - o If you are off-track, please provide a quick update on how you plan to get back on track. If further discussion is needed, take note to handle in a separate meeting.

Direct Report 1:1s

The purpose of a regular one-on-one meeting with your direct reports is to provide a dedicated time and space for you to connect with each team member individually. These meetings are typically scheduled on a regular basis (e.g., weekly or biweekly) and are focused on discussing topics that are relevant to each team member's work and career development.

Earlier in my career, when I first began managing people as part of my day-to-day workload, I didn't bother to create intentional time and space to have regular one-on-ones with the people I managed. Instead, I relied on ad hoc meetings, waiting until team members escalated something to me or simply bumped into me through the course of our days.

Perhaps unsurprisingly, this approach led to a backlog of unaddressed issues, causing people to underperform or feel unhappy. Then, when someone quit, it took me by surprise. It wasn't until years later—and some much-needed feedback from one of those team members who quit (see Geoff's story in Chapter 4)—that I began to understand this was a problem I'd created on my own.

These days, I give communication and retention much more thought. I have five direct reports—risk3sixty's team of C-suite executives—and treat each of my meetings with them as a can't-miss appointment. The way I see it, I have fifty opportunities over the course of a year to build rapport with each of these executives, and I am determined to seize every opportunity I can. These one-on-ones create space for my direct reports to bring issues to me. They are a safe place to have a deep, open, honest conversations—including conversations about personal issues. During my one-on-ones, I've learned about everything from problems on the team level to issues with underperformers to deaths in the family and personal crises. No matter what comes up, I'm always there to listen and give advice.

I know if I didn't have a track record of scheduling and showing up for these meetings consistently, I would not have the same rapport and history with my executives that I do—and therefore, they would not open up the way they do. Further, these meetings create communication clarity. Rather than schedule ad hoc meetings, my team members know that these one-on-ones are the perfect forum to surface issues.

These meetings can also be used to discuss each team member's career goals and aspirations. By understanding their career ambitions, I can help my team identify opportunities for growth and development within the organization.

Or, if they prefer, they can use these one-on-ones as a chance for us to simply be human together. After all, we're not robots. Our personal lives will naturally affect job performance, so it's important to talk about those issues when they arise.

The net result is a great relationship and lower turnover. When people do leave, neither party feels blindsided, because we've already talked about their situation, performance, plans, and other mitigating factors.

1:1 Agenda

Purpose

The purpose of this meeting is to review and prioritize top priorities for the individuals you manage directly.

Attendees

1:1 with direct reports

Duration

30 minutes to 1 hour

Agenda

- Good news, announcements, decisions made.
- Personal scorecard (e.g., family, health, events, etc.).
- Individual status:
  - Did you do what you said you would do last week?
  - What are you doing this week?
  - Any barriers to success?

1:1 Agenda (Continued)

- Status of big picture team goals
  - Present, on-track, or off-track status for each major goal.
  - If you are off-track, please provide a quick update on how you plan to get back on track. If further discussion is needed, take note to handle in a separate meeting.

Four Communication Tools

All right, I just want to acknowledge that I have already given you a whole chapter full of meeting cadence recommendations. My hope is that if you follow a disciplined regimen of meeting cadences, it will reduce the need for ad hoc meetings and result in fewer meetings for you overall. If you follow my recommendations exactly, you will have about 150 standing meetings on your calendar per year. That is less than one meeting per workday—can you imagine?

But I want to give you another set of my favorite tools to maximize your ability to help the team make decisions and get value out of meetings—or sometimes to avoid them altogether. My goal with these four communication protocols is to give you a handful of tools you can deploy when the situation calls.

Alternative #1. The Amazon Six-Pager

The story behind the Amazon Six-Pager can be traced back to the unique culture and leadership principles that define Amazon's approach to decision-making and communication. Amazon sought a method that would facilitate clear and concise communication while fostering critical thinking and informed decision-making.

The traditional approach of using lengthy slide deck presentations to convey ideas and proposals became a challenge at Amazon. The company found that presentations often lacked depth, failed to provide a comprehensive understanding of the problem and solution, and led to unproductive meetings with limited time for discussion and analysis.

To address these issues, Amazon introduced the concept of the six-pager. The six-pager format aimed to create a structured document that encapsulated the proposal, including relevant details, analysis, and recommendations, within a concise and focused narrative. This format ensured that ideas were thoroughly developed and articulated while allowing decision-makers to evaluate proposals more effectively.

By requiring teams to develop a comprehensive narrative document, Amazon ensured that proposals were grounded in deep understanding, data-driven analysis, and customer insights. This approach fostered critical thinking and encouraged teams to address potential risks and challenges proactively.

Moreover, the six-pager format promoted a culture of ownership and accountability. Each team member was responsible for developing and presenting their proposal in a clear, concise, and persuasive manner. This approach eliminated the need for excessive reliance on slide decks and encouraged individuals to take ownership of their ideas, driving the entrepreneurial spirit that defines Amazon's culture.

Over time, the Amazon six-pager became an integral part of the company's decision-making process, providing a framework for effective communication, empowering teams to think strategically, and enabling leaders to make informed decisions based on comprehensive analysis. The six-pager format continues to be a key tool for driving innovation, aligning stakeholders, and fostering a culture of customer-centric thinking within Amazon.

1. The structure of the Amazon six-pager typically consists of the following six sections:

2. **Executive summary:** This section provides a high-level overview of the proposal, summarizing the key points, objectives, and potential impact.

3. **Problem statement:** The problem statement identifies and defines the specific issue or opportunity that the proposal aims to address, clarifying why the problem is important, its impact on the business, and the need for a solution.

4. **Background and context:** This section provides relevant background information and context to help readers fully understand the proposal. It may include market analysis, customer insights, competitive landscape, and any other pertinent details.

5. **Proposal details:** Here, the proposal is outlined in detail. It includes the proposed solution, approach, and key features or initiatives. This section should be supported by data, research, and analysis to validate the feasibility and potential benefits of the proposal.

6. **Risks and mitigation strategies:** Identifying and addressing potential risks and challenges is crucial. This section highlights any risks associated with the proposal and offers mitigation strategies or contingency plans to minimize their impact.

7. **Recommendations and next steps:** The final section provides clear recommendations based on the proposal's analysis and evaluation. It outlines the next steps to be taken, including action plans, timelines, resource requirements, and key stakeholders involved.

At risk3sixty, we've adopted a version of the six-pager approach when designing proposals for our clients. Rather than trying to convince the company's whole chain of decision-makers to sit in on a presentation, we work with their CSO to build a compelling case for our program. Then, the CSO takes the document and disseminates it up the chain of command.

We've found a few key benefits to this approach. First, the process forces us and the CSO to organize our thinking ahead of time, to get clear on what we are proposing, and to highlight the value our partnership will bring. Second, at the very least, our six-pagers can reduce the overall meeting time to discuss our proposal. Instead of an hour-and-a-half conversation, for instance, we're in and out in thirty minutes. Sometimes, we're even able to bypass the meeting altogether.

While our version of the six-pager might not be out-and-out meeting replacement like it is at Amazon, we've found it to be an incredible time-saver that both forces us to articulate our ideas in the clearest way possible and improves communication up the decision-making chain.

Alternative #2. 37 Signal's Long-Form, Written, and Asynchronous

37signals is the maker of the Basecamp project management and Hey email platforms. Its founders, Jason Fried and David Heinemeier Hansson, are famous for their strong opinions about business and communication.

Jason and David have established thirty key principles of communication emphasizing that meetings are a last resort and written communication is strongly preferred. To uphold that philosophy, Jason and David recommend the following communications best practices:

- Internal communication based on long-form writing, rather than a verbal tradition of meetings, speaking, and chatting leads to a welcomed reduction in meetings, video conferences, calls, or other real-time opportunities to interrupt and be interrupted.

- Writing solidifies, chat dissolves. Substantial decisions start and end with an exchange of complete thoughts, not one-line-at-a-time jousts. If it's important, critical, or fundamental, write it up, don't chat it down.

- Write at the right time. Sharing something at 5 p.m. may keep someone at work longer. You may have some spare time on a Sunday afternoon to write something, but putting it out there on Sunday may pull people back into work on the weekends. Early Monday morning communication may be buried by other things. There may not be a perfect time, but there's certainly a wrong time. Keep that in mind when you hit send—and use the scheduling function on most email and messaging systems aggressively.

- Great news delivered on the heels of bad news makes both bits worse. The bad news feels like it's being buried, and the good news feels like it's being injected to change the mood. Be honest with each by giving each adequate space.[18]

37signals also relies on their collaboration platform Basecamp for communication rather than email, in-person, or instant messaging-based updates. For example, daily and weekly updates are based on automatic reminders in their collaboration portal. According to 37signals:

> Every Monday morning, Basecamp automatically asks everyone "What will you be working on this week?" This is a chance for everyone to lay out the big picture of their week. It's not about regurgitating individual tasks *or* diving headlong into the minutia of the week. It's generally just

---

[18] These bullets represent a few "rules of thumb," as outlined on Basecamp's website. For more, see: Basecamp. "The 37signals Guide to Internal Communication." Accessed December 3, 2023. https://basecamp.com/guides/how-we-communicate

your ten-thousand-foot view of the week ahead. The big picture items, the general themes. It sets your mind up for the work ahead, and, collectively, it gives everyone a good sense of what's happening across the company this week.[19]

37signals also asks every employee to reflect on their work every six weeks. The reflections, which they call heartbeats, are designed to give the whole company insight into the big picture accomplishments people are working on throughout each team:

> Heartbeats summarize the last ~6-weeks of work for a given team, department, or individual (if that person is a department of one). They're written by the lead of the group, and they're meant for everyone in the company to read. They summarize the big picture accomplishments, they detail the little things that mattered, and they generally highlight the importance of the work. They'll also shine a light on challenges and difficulties along the way. They're a good reminder that it's not all sunshine all the time. On balance, Heartbeats are wonderful to write, fun to read, and they help everyone—including those not directly involved with the work—reflect on jobs well done and progress well made.[20]

At risk3sixty, we've found great success in adapting 37signals's philosophy as part of our asynchronous communication strategy. As a hybrid company, we have a globally distributed workforce operating in several different time zones, making already-tedious update-based meetings even more inconvenient.

Instead, we focus on end-of-the-week updates using dedicated team channels on Slack. In these posts, each team member is required to give a brief update on where their projects stand, what they accomplished that week, and what they'll be focusing on in the next week.

If you're thinking that Friday afternoons are a strange time for these posts—after all, what if the team member provides bad news?—we thought of that too. These end-of-the-week posts aren't intended to send team members into the weekend fretting over whatever fresh disaster awaits them on Monday. In fact, they're meant create the exact opposite effect, to help team members get clarity on their week and clear their minds so they can enjoy the weekend unburdened.

---

[19] Ibid.
[20] Ibid.

As for the inevitable bad news, team members surface those issues well before Friday, thanks to the rest of the communication rhythms we've built in (see "Commander's Critical Information Requirements" later in the chapter). Team members know immediately how and when to escalate a challenge when it arises, and to keep their Friday updates high-level and strategically focused.

Alternative #3. Risk3sixty's Commander's Impact Filter

There are two communication concepts that I love. The military's "Commander's Intent" and Dan Sullivan's "Impact Filter."

In the military, the Commander's Intent is a concise and clear statement that communicates the purpose, desired end state, and key objectives of a mission or operation. It serves as the guiding principle for subordinate units and individual soldiers, ensuring they understand the commander's vision and can make informed decisions in the absence of detailed orders or in rapidly changing situations.

Similarly, Dan Sullivan's Impact Filter is a decision-making tool designed to help individuals and teams clarify their thinking, evaluate potential opportunities or projects, and make informed decisions by considering their desired impact and outcomes. The Impact Filter guides individuals through a series of questions to assess the viability and desirability of a specific idea or undertaking.

I combined these two formats to create my favorite written communication format: the Commander's Impact Filter. Leaders at risk3sixty are taught to use this format to add clarity to any projects before bringing them to the team.

For example, let's say I need to ask an analyst to conduct some research on a new cybersecurity regulation that may impact our clients. Instead of saying, "Can you go research the latest NIST framework?," I make the request in the format of a CIF to add clear purpose, priority, and clarity to the task. More importantly, by taking the time to structure my request in the form of a CIF, I show respect to the analyst and provide them with the appropriate guardrails to execute the assignment with freedom. The outcome is better, there is less frustration, and everyone wins.

The Commander's Impact Filter has these five elements:

Commander's Impact Filter

1. **Purpose:** I need you to do [x] by [date].

2. **Why this matters:** This initiative is important because [positive outcomes]. If you fail to do this, [negative outcomes].

3. **Task detail:**

Measure of success	[1 Measurable]
Roles	• Responsible: • Accountable: • Consulted: • Informed:
Communication plan	Please communicate to [party] via [method] on [frequency].
Required information	[Background information or needed information]
Objective	• **Objective Summary:** I need you to [do this] by [this date]. • **Measurable:** [add objective level measurable, if applicable] • **Tasks:** [Outline specifically what you want done]

Commander's Impact Filter (Continued)

4. Risk and mitigation measures:

Risks	• Describe any risks
How do we mitigate these risks?	• Describe ways we can mitigate these risks

5. **Desired end state:** At the conclusion of this initiative, we will have completed [objective]. We will know that we have succeeded because we have [1 measurable].

Alternative #4. The US Army's Commander's Critical Information Requirements (CCIR)

If you or your management team requires regular updates, provide specific guidance on how your team can streamline communication and help make sure that you have the right information, at the right time, and in the right format to make decisions. Often, this is much more efficient and clearer than a weekly in-person status meeting. A good tool for being clear with your team about what information you need is the Commander's Critical Information Requirements (CCIR).

In the military, CCIRs are specific pieces of information that the commander identifies as crucial for decision-making and situational awareness. They allow the commander to effectively plan, execute, and adapt to operational situations. In the context of your security team, they provide clear guidance on the specific data and details you need in your status updates.

For example, one CCIR used in the US Army is the mandate for immediate information regarding "enemy leadership location." Army officers know that if they obtain information regarding enemy leadership location, they are to report this information up the chain of command immediately.

This approach is how we avoid status bombs during our Friday updates. Team members know that if something is off, that is command-critical information and should be escalated immediately.

Critical information requirements promote consistency and standardization in urgent status updates. They ensure that everyone on the team understands the specific data and metrics that need to be included, allowing for easier comparison and analysis across different updates and periods. Further, they facilitate effective communication and reporting within your team. When team members know what information is critical to include, they can provide concise, relevant, and meaningful updates. This promotes efficient communication and enables you to quickly grasp the key information and insights.

Critical information requirements enable data-driven decision-making. When the necessary data and metrics are consistently included in the status updates, you have access to the information needed to assess progress, identify trends, make informed decisions, and take timely actions to address any issues or risks. They also promote accountability and performance management. When team members know the specific information they are expected to provide, it fosters a sense of responsibility and ownership. Finally, the standardized format of critical information requirements allows leaders to objectively track progress, evaluate performance, and provide targeted feedback based on the critical information included in the team member's updates.

Every team will have different criteria for determining their CCIRs. Think through what information you would like to be escalated and in what format. A few common examples to consider:

- Health of the security program or elements of the security program
- Status of a project or key milestone
- Team member performance
- Matters of health and safety
- Financial issues over a certain monetary threshold

To make sure your team provides the right information at the right time for every pillar of your security program, here is a CCIR format you can use:

Commander's Critical Information Requirements (CCIR)

1. **Purpose:** I need this information update because [x].

2. **Why this matters:** This initiative is important because [positive outcomes]. If you fail to do this [negative outcomes].

3. **Cadence of communication:** I need this information [time] in [format].

4. **Information required:** In the update please include [describe information].

5. **Decision points:** Decision points are key events or milestones in the operational timeline where the leader must make critical decisions. These decision points may require specific information to assess the situation accurately and determine the best course of action.

   a. If any of the following conditions are met, I will need to be notified immediately for a decision [describe conditions].
   b. Please notify me upon [milestone].

Every Problem is a Communication Problem

Here's the bottom line: most of the problems on your team are communication problems.

If your team is frustrated by decisions made by management—communication problem. If your team doesn't understand the intended outcome of a project—communication problem. If your team can't make decisions without you—communication problem.

And if you have too many communication problems, bad things happen. Rumors prevail over truth, confusion about goals hinders decision-making, and performance is doomed. A leader cannot manage a team if communication is broken.

But if you implement the communication rhythms outlined in this chapter, your team will have the clarity it needs to perform with confidence.

- Annual and quarterly meetings will serve as consistent big-picture reminders of what your team needs to accomplish.
- Quarterly IRC and IRB meetings will ensure important decisions are made in a timely manner.
- Weekly all-hands and sub-team meetings will serve as week-in and week-out information dissemination tools to keep everyone on the same page.
- One-on-ones will create an intimate space to work out issues.

That is the power of the Security Team Operating System.

As George Bernard Shaw once said, "The single biggest problem in communication is the illusion that it has taken place." By organizing your team around set, repeatable rhythms, you can guarantee that communication actually *will* take place.

Download the Tools

Download the tools referenced in this chapter to document your team's Rhythms at www.risk3sixty.com/stos

Download it by scanning this (you won't regret it)

CHAPTER 6

GOALS

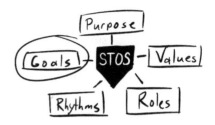

Executive Summary

Leaders harness the team's energy to accomplish a clear objective. In this chapter, we will cover how leaders can align their team's priorities to accomplish their defined objectives. First, we will explore tools to ensure business objectives, security team objectives, and individual goals are harmonized. Then, we will cover real-world examples as well as tools to set, track, and hold the team accountable to the goals they sign up for.

Self-Assessment Questions

☐	What are the key objectives for your company this year?
☐	What are the key objectives for your security team this year?
☐	Are the objectives of your security team clearly mapped to the objectives of the company?
☐	Does each individual have specific and measurable goals?
☐	Do individual goals align to the team's objective?
☐	How are your team members held accountable to achieving their goals?
☐	How do you know if your team members are hitting or missing their goals?

There's a famous story about an investor who visited the manufacturing floor at SpaceX. Seeing a SpaceX employee assembling a large part, he stopped to ask him, "What is your job here?"

The employee answered, "The mission of SpaceX is to colonize Mars. In order to colonize Mars, we need to build reusable rockets because it will otherwise be unaffordable for humans to travel to Mars and back. My job is to help design the steering system that enables our rockets to land back on Earth. You'll know if I've succeeded if our rockets land on our platform in the Atlantic after launch."

What a great example of purpose-to-goal alignment.

If your CEO were to ask one of your security analysts about their job, could they tie their work back to the business's objective? Or would they stumble through it?

The kind of clarity seen by the employees at SpaceX might not seem obtainable, but that's the power of a well-defined security team operating system. It ties the big picture vision of the company to the security team's vision down to individual goals.

Clarity creates focused energy.

To understand how this works, think of a symphony orchestra. In a symphony, every musician is tasked with playing the same song. Although each player's sheet of music is unique to them, when they combine their efforts, the orchestra is in harmony together, and together they produce a beautiful, dynamic piece of music.

This is precisely what happens at SpaceX and among other high-performing teams. Your team must have a common objective with each person's individual goals harmonized to accomplish a broader mission.

As the leader, it is your job to create that harmony. You are the conductor, orchestrating an entire group of professionals around a single goal. For an orchestra, that goal is the successful performance of a song or symphony. For you, that goal is the business and security objectives that your team sets out to accomplish.

Here in the final step of the Security Team Operating System, we're coming full circle, examining the role of goals in the purpose-to-goals framework and how you can leverage them to help your team produce tremendous results. First, we'll discuss the importance of setting focused goals (and what happens if you don't), and then we'll spend the rest of the chapter taking a deep dive into the goal setting process.

What Happens When You Don't Set Focused Goals

At risk3sixty, we have always been pretty good about setting goals. Every year, we set firm goals, then we ask each department to set goals that align with the company's goals. Each department manager works with their team to set individual goals that support their team. We then track all of those goals in our performance management tool and revisit progress toward goals each quarter at our quarterly team review.

But for the first five years, we did not have a good process to help individuals set goals in alignment with what the company was trying to accomplish. So, people would set goals that didn't help the firm accomplish anything. For example, in one instance, we had a team member set a personal goal to renovate their house. That was a great goal, and I am happy that person was focused on improving their life, but it had nothing to do with helping us accomplish our company's mission.

Sometimes a person's individual goals even work against the larger strategy of the company. For instance, we had a department head set a goal to research an outsourced payroll provider. That was a great idea, but not a firm priority. As a result, they wasted a lot of time and company energy on a second- or third-tier goal.

None of this misalignment was intentional, of course. Our team members' hearts were in the right place. It's just that we didn't have a good system to harness the team's collective energy to accomplish a singular mission.

Our goal setting system was broken, resulting in a lot of wasted energy.

The other problem we had was that people would set too many goals. Some ambitious team members would set ten or twenty goals for the year, when three to five goals would have more than sufficed. As thought leader Karen Martin said, "When everything is a priority, nothing is a priority."[21] Setting too many goals divided our team members' attention and spread their energy too thin to be effective. People who try to push too many goals at once usually wind up doing a mediocre job on all of them—or worse, not completing any of them.

The solution to these challenges is a system to harness the team's energy around a single, clear objective. If you can do that, your team can accomplish anything together.

Purpose to Goals Alignment

Set the Right Team Objective

In Chapter 2, we talked about setting your team's purpose. Establishing a clear purpose in alignment with the company's objectives is an important first step for successful team and individual goal setting. If you haven't set a clear purpose yet, consider rereading Chapter 2 and doing the exercises. This will help you get a clear and measurable objective out of your head and on paper. This is an important step because once you have established a clear purpose, you can communicate it to your team and begin aligning your team's goals to accomplish it.

One other thing: Don't put too much pressure on yourself. No objective is perfect. And it doesn't have to be. It just needs to be good enough. It needs to be clear. And the whole team needs to understand it. It is better for the whole team to be moving 100 percent toward an objective that is only 70 percent accurate than for the leader to fail to set an objective at all.

Here are the minimum criteria for setting an objective:

- The security team's objective must be in alignment with the company's objective.
- The objective must be documented.
- The objective must be clearly communicated and understood by all team members.

---

[21] Karen Martin. *The Outstanding Organization: Generate Business Results by Eliminating Chaos and Building the Foundation for Everyday Excellence.* (New York: McGraw Hill) 2012.

Of course, just because the criteria are fairly straightforward doesn't mean they're easy to implement. As you'll see in the next section, communication alone is a nonstop effort.

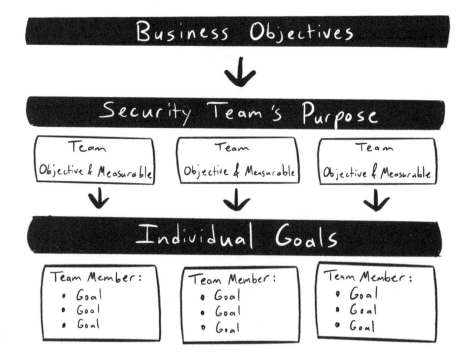

Clearly Communicate the Objective

Setting a clear objective is the first step. Then you have to communicate it. This is where many leaders go wrong.

Creating an objective is about 20 percent of the work. The other 80 percent of the work is communicating that objective to your team. It is your job to make sure your team understands the objective, buys into it, and can communicate it to the people they manage. Just like you, all of your leaders must be on repeat.

The Marketing Rule of 7

In marketing, there is a commonly held belief that a prospective customer needs to be exposed to a marketing message or brand at least seven times before they are inclined to act or make a purchase decision. This time-honored axiom accounts for the psychological phenomenon of familiarity and the time it takes for an individual to develop trust and confidence in a product or service.

The same principle applies to leaders communicating new concepts and objectives to their team. Leaders need to be on repeat, restating the team's objective every chance they get—in meetings, in one-on-ones, in presentations, in reports, in slogans on the wall, in metrics. The objective should be everywhere.

Every year, we set new objectives at risk3sixty. Here is how the process works:

- **August:** Off-site meeting for brainstorming.
- **August–October:** Establish draft budget, firm targets, themes, and strategic objectives.
- **October:** Present draft plan to our management team.
- **October–December:** Refine and finalize strategic plan.
- **January:** Present plan to the team at the annual team off-site.

The reason I am providing this timeline is to point out that by the time the full team is presented our strategic plan (in January), I have been working on the strategic plan for five months. By the time we roll it out to our teams, I know the strategic plan backward and forward. I have all of the context of how we arrived at the plan, I've seen the math, and I have had all of the nuanced discussions.

But it is the first time my team has heard it.

That means I have to have the patience and empathy to clearly explain our plan to my team . . . at least six more times! As a security leader, you will experience the same phenomena. You will experience communication fatigue, and you will get frustrated. And that's okay. It is normal. When I am feeling frustrated, I remember a quote from renowned business coach Gino Wickman:

> People need to hear the vision seven times before they really hear it for the first time. Human beings have short attention spans and are a little jaded when it comes to new messages. As a good leader, you must remain consistent in your message.[22]

---

[22] Gino Wickman. *Traction: Get a Grip on Your Business.* (Dallas: BenBella Books). 2012.

7 Opportunities to Communicate Your Objective

If you are looking for inspiration, here are seven effective ways to communicate your objective:

1. Present your objective at the annual team meeting.
2. Present progress toward the objective at quarterly team updates.
3. Present progress metrics toward the objective at every weekly team meeting.
4. Talk about progress toward the objective during 1:1s.
5. Ensure the team sets individual goals in alignment with the security team's objectives. (Many performance review platforms have this capability.)
6. Laminate your objective and hand it out to the teams as a one-page reminder.
7. Incorporate your objective into the orientation materials for new team members.

The Goal Setting Process

Now that you feel confident that the security team's objective is understood by all, the next is to ensure that the whole team is setting and meeting goals in alignment with that objective. In the following discussion, I'll show you how you to harness the energy of the entire team around a single objective.

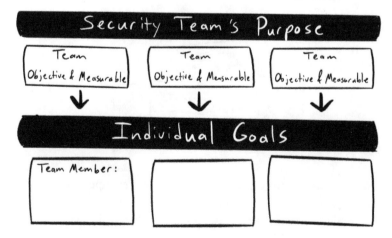

How to Set Goals

My work has taken me to some interesting places. Once, it even took me to the center of a literal mine. Traveling to the center of the mine wasn't originally on our agenda, and it had little to do with our work helping the company's security team, but I'm a firm believer that if someone asks you if you want to see the inside of a mine, the only proper answer is a resounding "yes!"

Inside the mine, our guide explained to us the intricacies of blasting rock for maximum utility. To do that, he held up a small amount of C-4, no larger than a quarter. Depending on how it was applied to the tunnel wall, that small amount of C-4 could have wildly different results.

Applied superficially, it would barely have an impact on the rocks it was intended to blast. Applied strategically in the form of a shaped charge, it could do an incredible amount of damage. Why?

Focused energy.

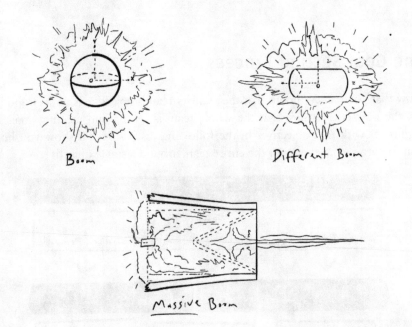

Boom

Different Boom

Massive Boom

The is the same with setting goals. You can either set superficial goals or you can set strategic goals that focus energy to accomplish a clear mission. Leaders often set ambiguous goals, such as "become a better leader" or "obtain a certification." They have good intentions, but their goals are too ambiguous to be helpful.

Misdirected goals may not help accomplish a key objective, or worse, they may even detract from that objective. For example, we had one team member who set a goal to become more involved in a local chapter of a security organization. Historically, this person had been a very talented team member and contributed at an elite level, but we noticed they started missing deadlines and key deliverables.

After a coaching meeting, we found out that the team member had been asked to take a major volunteer role at the security organization and were working twenty to thirty hours per week in that volunteer position. It was a well-intended goal, but ultimately it was misdirected energy, detracting from that person's performance, their passion, and the organization's objective.

We work with team members and security leaders to be more strategic with their goals so that they can have the greatest impact. For every goal someone suggests, we ask:

- What business objective does this help accomplish?
- Why did you set this goal personally?
- What specific leadership skill are you trying to improve, and why?
- What resources do you need to accomplish this goal?
- How will you know if you have accomplished it?

Usually, this leads to a much more refined—and a much more impactful—goal. Instead of "Become a better leader," for instance, the new, adjusted goal might be "Improve my leadership skills by focusing on my ability to clearly communicate expectations and hold team members accountable."

This is the kind of goal setting necessary to create a high-performing security team. Collaborating with your team to formulate meaningful goals is a strategic imperative that cultivates a culture of clarity, engagement, and purpose-driven performance. By involving team members in the goal setting process, you tap into their expertise and insights, creating a collective vision that resonates deeply with their individual aspirations. This approach fosters a sense of ownership, as team members become active contributors to the goals they help shape. This heightened engagement then translates into increased motivation, commitment, and collaboration, since individuals are more likely to invest effort in goals that they have cocreated.

It is difficult to help your team accomplish ambiguous goals. It leaves too much room for misinterpretation. Ambiguity in goal setting can lead team members to interpret objectives differently, resulting in misaligned efforts. A lack of clarity can also make it challenging to gauge success or measure progress accurately, leading to more confusion as team members struggle to discern what exactly is expected of them. Holding people accountable becomes almost impossible.

Without a well-defined framework, the team's focus can scatter, with each team member prioritizing different aspects or pursuing divergent paths—undermining overall coherence. Ambiguous goals can also weaken accountability, as it's challenging to hold individuals responsible for outcomes that are not precisely articulated.

SMART Goals

If you want to set clear goals, I suggest the SMART method. The SMART method is a popular framework for setting goals that are Specific, Measurable, Achievable, Relevant, and Time-bound. Here's a breakdown of each component and how to effectively set goals using the SMART method:

- **Specific:** Clearly define the goal. Make it as detailed and focused as possible. Avoid vague or general statements by asking yourself the "W" questions: What do I want to accomplish? Why is it important? Who is involved? Where will it happen?

- **Measurable:** Set criteria to measure your progress and determine when the goal is achieved. Establish quantifiable indicators to track your progress. This helps in assessing your journey and ensuring you're on the right track. Consider questions like: How much? How many? How will I know when I've accomplished the goal?

- **Achievable:** Ensure that the goal is realistic and attainable given your current resources, skills, and circumstances. Aim high, but make sure the goal isn't so far-fetched that it becomes demotivating. Consider whether the goal is within your control and whether it aligns with your capabilities.

- **Relevant:** Ensure the goal aligns with your broader objectives, whether they are personal, team-related, or organizational. Goals should contribute meaningfully to your overall mission and priorities. Ask

160

yourself whether the goal is worthwhile and whether it fits into your bigger picture.

- **Time-bound:** Set a specific deadline for achieving the goal. Establishing a timeframe creates a sense of urgency and helps prevent procrastination. Consider when you want to achieve the goal and whether it's realistically achievable within that time frame.

To give you an example of a SMART goal in action, imagine you're a CISO seeking to enhance your team's cybersecurity skills, a SMART goal might be:

Within the next six months, provide cybersecurity training to all team members (Specific and Measurable) to improve their ability to identify and mitigate potential threats (Relevant). This goal is achievable within the given timeframe and aligns with the team's development needs (Achievable and Time-bound).

By applying the SMART method, you transform vague aspirations into well-defined, actionable objectives. This approach fosters clarity, accountability, and an increased likelihood of success in achieving your goals.

How to Hold People Accountable

Most of us probably set goals to lose weight every year. We get a gym membership, then never go to the gym. We set a diet plan, then fall off the wagon. That's because most of us skip an important step: creating a system of accountability.

Accountability helps you stay committed by creating transparency, responsibility, and measurable progress. It helps ensure that goals remain at the forefront of your focus and that someone is there to call you out if you start getting off track. Perhaps most importantly, accountability fosters a sense of ownership, where the individual becomes personally invested in the outcomes they seek to attain; they have skin in the game that creates consequences for quitting.

Involving others in the process, whether colleagues, mentors, or coaches, provides an external layer of support and scrutiny. This added dimension drives motivation, encourages consistent effort, and discourages complacency.

For example, I knew that if I wanted to get this book done, I would need to build some accountability into the process. It takes one to two years of consistent writing, editing, and revising to complete a project like this. So, I hired a great editor, Chas Hoppe, to help hold me accountable. For months, Chas helped me set deadlines and goals to finish the book. Just knowing that I had someone to report to kept me honest during the process.

That is the main reason people have better results if they use a personal trainer. Maybe you will skip the gym if you are on your own, but you are more likely to show up if you know someone is counting on you to be there. We all do better when we have someone counting on us for the result. Your team members want an accountability partner—and that accountability partner is *you.*

Build Accountability into Your Rhythms—Tying It All Together

First, let's acknowledge the elephant in the room: holding someone accountable is a lot of work.

But while it may be a lot of work, the process itself is straightforward. In fact, we already covered the best way to do it in Chapter 5: build the practice into your existing rhythms.

If you look back at that chapter, you will notice that each sample meeting agenda already has a placeholder to both make commitments and check-in on them. That is accountability in practice.

So, set expectations, get a commitment, and follow up. It will feel like a lot sometimes, but at least the process is simple.

Jack Stack's System of Accountability

One of my favorite examples of a system of accountability comes from thought leader Jack Stack's book *The Great Game of Business.* Stack's system revolves around the principles of open-book management and creating a culture of ownership and transparency within the organization, focusing on three key things:

Transparency and Education

At the core of Stack's approach is the practice of open-book management, where all employees are educated about the key drivers of the business. This includes sharing critical business objectives, goals, and key performance indicators (KPIs). To ensure effective participation, Stack emphasizes the need to educate employees at all levels on how to understand and interpret their KPIs. This empowers them to make informed decisions that positively impact the company's performance.

Aligning Incentives

Stack believes that when employees have a stake in the company's success, they are more motivated to contribute to its growth. This is achieved by implementing an incentive program that links individual and team performance to the company's results.

An essential component of Stack's system is the implementation of a gain-sharing bonus plan. When the company achieves its financial targets, a portion of the profits is distributed among employees, providing them with a tangible reward for their contributions.

As a security leader, you might not be able to implement a bonus system, but most likely you can think of a few other incentives to encourage participation—such as tying successful goal completion to promotions or raises.

Help Set the Goals to Drive Buy-In

Stack is a master at driving buy-in from his team. The way he does this is by getting his employees to help design the team's goals and objectives themselves. Of course, he is there to guide them, but he is aware that his team is much more likely to buy into goals that they create themselves.

Employees are involved in setting both short-term and long-term goals, aligning their targets with the company's overall objectives. These goals are specific, measurable, achievable, relevant, and time-bound (SMART) to ensure clarity and accountability. To help hold people accountable, Stack recommends regular weekly meetings to review progress, share financial updates, and discuss any challenges or opportunities. These huddles foster transparency, collaboration, and a collective effort toward achieving organizational goals.

Stack's system of accountability focuses on fostering a sense of ownership, transparency, and business acumen among employees. By involving them in the decision-making process and providing them with a stake in the company's success, this approach helps to drive overall performance and achieve sustainable growth.

Remember Where You're Headed

Let me tell you about a time I failed.

It was late 2023. For the past couple of years, we had been working with a highly regulated technology company who engaged risk3sixty to manage their security compliance program. We had just helped guide them through a slew of security certifications for the first time and were celebrating a big win for them. After a full year of effort, we finally crossed the finish line. It felt great.

And then they fired us.

Confused, I called a meeting with the CEO. "Look, I'm not mad that you fired us. It's your company and your call," I said. "But I am trying to understand why. Founder to founder, I'm asking you to level with me. What did we do wrong?"

"You were working against me," the CEO said.

As he explained, the company was preparing to be acquired. This was a rare win-win for everyone involved. The owners were going to get paid, the employees were about to get huge raises and great new benefits, and the customers were going to upgrade into a new ecosystem.

But our team had no idea.

We thought we were there to help the client mature their cybersecurity program, to treat it as if it was supposed to exist forever. In service of that goal, we introduced new initiatives, outlined the processes for next steps and additional certifications, and laid out guidelines for expanding roles and staffing up their team. We were building a great program that would take the company to the next level.

But that wasn't their goal. That's not what a company preparing for an acquisition wants or needs.

What the owner really needed from us was to reduce cost and complexity, help drive profits as high as possible, and create an easy-to-migrate compliance program to hand off to the acquiring company. We didn't know that, so we didn't do that.

Instead, we were operating like maturity was the mission. Everything we were doing made sense given our understood objectives. However, in context of the client's *actual* objectives, the owner was right: we were working against them.

If I were him, in the face of such gross misalignment, I would have fired us too.

Now, the situation wasn't entirely our fault. When the company first joined us as a client, maturity *was* their goal. But somewhere along the way, the goal changed, we weren't notified, and we failed to discover this shift in priorities ourselves.

But we could have. In fact, we even had clearly defined processes intended to flush out precisely this kind of information. But, with the benefit of hindsight, I could see that we didn't follow the playbook closely enough—and as a result, we lost a good client.

Were we to run the clock back and get a second chance, we would have worked harder to define and attach ourselves to the business's primary objective. We should have set security team objectives to support the client's objectives. We should have set individual goals to keep everyone aligned. We should have run our program so that the client had no choice but to update us on their shifting priorities.

But while hindsight is twenty-twenty, I'm giving you the chance to see into the future to prevent this kind of mistake from happening to your organization. As we learned the hard way, you can set all the well-intentioned goals in the world, but if they're not aligned with your business objectives, then you risk working against your own company.

Ask yourself:

- Do you know exactly where your company is headed and why?
- Is your security team's vision aligned with the business's?
- Are your team's individual goals aligned?

If not, you have a huge opportunity sitting right in front of you.

Be clear. Be focused. Harness the team's energy. And you will accomplish great things.

Download the Tools

Download the tools referenced in this chapter to document your team's Goals at www.risk3sixty.com/stos

CHAPTER 7

GET STARTED NOW

Executive Summary

Now it is time to put the STOS into practice. In this chapter, we will cover the immediate next steps you can take to make progress on implementing the STOS.

Step 1: Schedule a Think Day

Right now, you are probably overwhelmed with ideas you are excited to implement. To get all of your thoughts organized, schedule a think day. A think day can be a valuable tool to help you gain clarity and assist with planning for your cybersecurity team. It will allow you to step back from your daily tasks and responsibilities and focus on some much-needed introspection. Use this time to reflect on your current cybersecurity strategies, challenges, and goals, allowing you to gain a deeper understanding of the situation and identify any areas that need improvement.

Schedule your think day somewhere off-site. My favorite place to have a think day is my local coffee shop. It is a place I can settle in and think deeply. You might also consider getting a cabin, checking into a hotel, or visiting a shared workspace. Just make sure it is somewhere you can work creatively and undisturbed. At the office, it is common to be constantly interrupted by meetings, emails, and other distractions. You need uninterrupted time to focus solely on your STOS.

If I'm being honest, though, a think day will not be enough. Instead, consider an entire think week as part of your standard planning process. I recommend that you spend a third of your time thinking deeply, a third of your time relaxing and enjoying leisure activities, and a third of your time doing something fun.

Spending your time this way might feel like a free vacation, but it is not. Numerous studies show that relaxing and having fun are essential parts of creativity and deep thinking. In other words, this "vacation time" is absolutely critical for your team.

I schedule an annual "clarity break" for personal and professional planning. I usually rent a cabin for a few days and spend time thinking, hiking, and reading books that spark creativity. This is my way of letting my brain relax and reach peak creativity. As a result, I always bring back fresh ideas for my team and my family. It makes a huge difference in the quality of ideas I can bring to the table. The investment of time and money also acts as a forcing mechanism to take the opportunity seriously. I force myself not to waste time and to make the most of the opportunity.

Bill Gates, cofounder of Microsoft, is famous for his own "think weeks." When he was CEO of Microsoft, Gates took a week-long retreat *twice a year* to seclude himself in a cabin and immerse himself in reading, thinking, and reflecting on various topics related to technology and Microsoft's future.

Bill Gates used these weeks as uninterrupted time to step away from his daily responsibilities, meetings, and distractions so he could explore new ideas, examine emerging technologies, and consider his long-term vision for Microsoft. During these think weeks, Gates would read and review technical papers, research reports, industry trends, and other innovative ideas.

These "think week papers," as they came to be called, were written by Microsoft employees who had the opportunity to submit their proposals, ideas, and insights directly to Gates. The papers themselves covered a wide range of topics, including software development, technological advancements, business strategies, and potential future directions for Microsoft.

Step 2: Download and Complete the Security Team Operating System Templates and Workbook

Throughout this book, we have referenced templates to help put these concepts into action. We have also created the Security Team Operating System Workbook. You can use the templates and workbook to brainstorm about the concepts in this book during your think day or think week.

Below you will find a list of all of the templates for quick reference:

Download the Tools

Download all of the tools in this book!

Step 3: Ask Your Team to Read This Book

Remember, this whole journey is about harnessing your team's energy to accomplish an important objective. To spark lasting change on your team, you need to bring everyone on this journey with you so they can be just as energized by the idea of implementing the concepts in this book as you. They need to understand why you want to undertake this work and what they need to do—all while using the same language and toolsets.

At risk3sixty, we first rolled out the operating systems I have detailed in this book in 2020. My goal at the time was to begin the journey of creating a better-running company where each business unit ran on a common system using a common language. I started by creating and documenting an operating system for the company itself so the business unit leaders could emulate it.

However, I did not do a good job of explaining to the team the *why* behind the *what* that I was asking them to do. As a result, the operating system at each business unit level looked very different, had varying degrees of quality, and was not well understood by the team members who reported to each business unit.

It wasn't until I clearly documented the STOS (using the Commander's Intent format outlined in Chapter 5) and did several training sessions with our management team that they bought in. Today, each of our business units has a STOS documented and shared in our internal wiki. The STOS is understood by all and updated annually as part of our strategic planning cadence. As a leader, I have a lot of confidence that our team is on the same page, using the same language, and rowing in the same direction. We have used the STOS framework to harness the team's energy to accomplish business unit and company goals that help us accomplish our purpose.

As Andrew Carnegie said, "Teamwork is the ability to work together toward a common vision. The ability to direct individual accomplishments toward organizational objectives. It is the fuel that allows common people to attain uncommon results."

Remember to bring your team along with you for this journey. You won't regret it.

Step 4: Schedule Your Annual Off-Site

I find that most people work best when there is a clear deadline ahead. To drive action, go ahead and get your annual off-site onto the calendar. Book the location and tell your team about it. This commitment will act as an accountability checkpoint to implement the STOS. (You can use the annual off-site agenda in chapter 5 as a starting point.)

For Fun, Think Big

I also encourage you to think big. Consider what this meeting could be and what it could represent for your team. This could be the type of meeting that your team never forgets. It could be the event they look forward to every year. It could be a meeting you use to harness the team's energy to accomplish the biggest goals you have ever set for the organization. Obviously, your annual meeting doesn't have to hit these types of lofty goals, but it is fun and motivating to challenge yourself to this standard.

Here are some fun ideas we have tried in the past:

- Rented cabins and held the event in the mountains of North Georgia.
- Picked the team up in a party bus and drove them to an off-site location at a comedy club. We had the off-site meeting at the comedy club during the day, and then as a team event, we watched a show that evening.
- Watched an elaborate demo of new product and dashboard features that were going to make our team's life a lot better. (If you need inspiration, check out Steve Job's big product release demos of the MAC or iPhone.)
- Created and decorated poster boards for each team with their top three team goals. We hung the posters on the wall as a reminder of what we wanted to accomplish.

Keep the Main Thing the Main Thing

In his book *The 7 Habits of Highly Effective People,* author Stephen Covey reminds us to "Keep the main thing the main thing." Indeed, he is correct. Remember that the most important element of your meeting cadences is to harness your team's energy to accomplish an important mission. *That mission is the main thing.*

The purpose of fun off-site meetings is primarily to capture the attention of your team so they can focus on the important message you're there to deliver. If your annual meeting accomplishes that, you have done your job. You do not have to blow out the budget. You do not have to deliver a Steve Jobs-style talk. You just need to get everyone on the same page about what's important. Have fun, but do not put too much pressure on yourself. *Keep the main thing the main thing.*

Go. Go now. Get your annual meeting on the calendar!

Step 5: Get Help

Becoming great requires help. Don't believe me? Just look at this quote from legendary sports trainer Tim Grover:

> Do. The. Work. Every day, you have to do something you don't want to do. Every day. Challenge yourself to be uncomfortable, push past the apathy and laziness and fear. Otherwise, the next day you're going to have two things you don't want to do, then three and four and five, and pretty soon, you can't even get back to the first thing. And then all you can do is beat yourself up for the mess you've created, and now you've got a mental barrier to go along with the physical barriers.[23]

Why should you listen to Tim Grover? Because this is the same advice he gave to all-time great sports icons like Michael Jordan, Kobe Bryant, and Dwyane Wade. His training playbook and methodologies turn great athletes into legendary icons.

Tim Grover trained Michael Jordan for over fifteen years. Grover first started working with Jordan in 1989 when Jordan hired him as his personal trainer during his prime years with the Chicago Bulls. Tim helped Michael Jordan reach peak performance and stay there for over a decade.

Grover pushed Jordan to his limits and designed customized workout regimens that targeted specific areas for improvement. Their training sessions were known for their intensity and dedication to pushing boundaries. Beyond physical training, Grover also played a vital role in Jordan's mental preparation. He helped Jordan develop a winning mindset and the mental toughness required to perform under pressure. Grover's approach focused on eliminating distractions, building confidence, and instilling an unyielding determination to succeed.

Their collaboration produced remarkable results. During their time together, Jordan won six NBA championships, five MVP awards, and numerous scoring titles. Jordan's ability to dominate the game, especially during crucial moments, was a testament to the physical and mental conditioning instilled by Grover.

---

[23] Tim S. Grover. *Relentless: From Good to Great to Unstoppable.* (New York: Scribner): 2013.

Who is Your Tim Grover?

No one operates at an elite level without the help of a coach and accountability partners. Now that you've read *Security Team Operating System*, here is how you can continue your growth and learn to develop and lead a world-class security team:

- **Coaching and STOS workshop:** Using a coach to implement a security program is like using an elite personal trainer to achieve a new level of fitness. At risk3sixty, our team has helped some of the best security leaders in the industry level up their security program and harness the energy of their team to accomplish important goals. If you want to achieve a new level of results, schedule one of our workshops for your team. Our workshops create dedicated time and space so you can think about strategy in a product format. We pull from experience with hundreds of organizations and leverage a tested step-by-step playbook to create better results. Check out https://risk3sixty.com/stos for more information.

- **Tackle security and compliance together:** Maybe you are so burdened with the day-to-day you can't get your head above water long enough to think about strategy and team building. An endless barrage of audits, recurring tasks, board meetings, security incidents, gathering more audit evidence, plus your day job. We get it. That is why we offer Compliance and Compliance-as-a-Service offerings to operate as an extension of your team to build and manage your program on your behalf. Our Compliance-as-a-Service playbook, supported by a purpose-built GRC platform, helps take the operational burden of security teams so you can focus on strategy, risk management, and building relationships internally. If you want GRC and compliance done for and with you, this is an excellent option.

- **Free videos, templates, and thought leadership:** We have spent thousands of hours creating free videos, templates, and thought leadership to help security and GRC teams take their programs to the next level. We have practical templates for budgets, presentations at the board level, and a multi-part video series on building security programs all available for free.

ACKNOWLEDGMENTS

Thank you to my family for giving me the time, space, and encouragement to write this book: Lauren, Lily, Benjamin, and Sonora. I understand that when Dad is sitting in front of his computer on Saturday mornings, it is not just work for me, but also for you. Thank you.

To my mother, Sonya Hyatt, who instilled in me an unreasonable confidence as a child. That confidence set a foundation to take shots like starting a business and writing a book. Unconditional love is a rare thing, but I have that gift from you. Thank you.

Harry and Becky. I love you guys and thank you for always being there. There is a certain comfort in knowing someone will always be there for you. For over twenty years you guys have been that for me.

The ideas in this book aren't just ideas. They are put into practice every day at risk3sixty. Thank you to my business partner and risk3sixty co-founder, Christian White, for the brainstorming sessions, the encouragement, and the partnership over the last decade. The concepts in this book are as much yours as they are mine.

Many of my beliefs about business have been shaped by guides and mentors. Thank you to my unofficial mastermind group, most of which I have only met in books, who have had significant influence on my thinking to this point: Gino Wickman, Verne Harnish, Patrick Lencioni, Jack Stack, Rob Campbell, Jason Fried, David Maister, Dan Sullivan, Felix Denis, and many more.

I could not have completed this book without the partnership of my editor, Chas Hoppe and book designer, Timmy Bauer. Thank you for the help getting this over the finish line.

When I was short of mentors, I found them on the wrestling mat. Thank you to my high school wrestling coach Kelby W. for being a mentor to young men for the past several decades. You may never know the full impact you have made on so many.

God. Your will is a mystery. But, over time I hope that I do a better job listening. Listening as much with my heart as with my head. Thank you for every experience in life required to get to this point.

ABOUT THE AUTHOR

Christian is widely considered one of the foremost experts on cybersecurity, GRC, and compliance around the globe. Renowned as a highly regarded keynote speaker and thought leader, Christian has worked with entrepreneurs, CEOs, corporate executives, and security experts across the world.

As the CEO and Co-founder of risk3sixty, Christian's team helps many of the world's leading technology organizations assess, build, and manage security programs challenged with compliance initiatives like SOC 2, ISO 27001, PCI DSS, HITRUST, FedRAMP, and penetration testing.

Under Christian's leadership, risk3sixty has been named Consulting Magazine's Best Firms to Work For, Fastest Growing companies, Best Places to Work, and HireVets Platinum Honoree, and Top 100 CEOs by Titan 100.

Christian has an M.B.A. from Georgia Tech and a B.B.A. from the University of Georgia where he currently serves as a Georgia Tech Technology and Management (T&M) corporate partner and Advisory Board Member for UGA's Management Information System Advisory Board.